CHINOOKS IN THE DARK

I dedicate this book to my Grandchildren. When I first went to war, my sons were young, and through my experiences, I never thought I'd live long enough to enjoy the company of their offspring: Cason, Annalea, Merritt, Adalyne, and Aiden. They bring a smile every time I'm with them.

CHINOOKS IN THE DARK

MH-47S, AND THE 160TH SOAR NIGHT STALKERS

ALAN C. MACK

Pen & Sword
MILITARY
AN IMPRINT OF PEN & SWORD BOOKS LTD.
YORKSHIRE – PHILADELPHIA

First published in Great Britain in 2026 by
PEN AND SWORD MILITARY
An imprint of
Pen & Sword Books Limited
Yorkshire – Philadelphia

Print ISBN 978 1 39907 920 4
ePUB ISBN 978 1 39907 922 8
ePDF ISBN 978 1 39907 924 2

A CIP catalogue record for this book is available from the British Library.

Typeset in 12/15 Ehrhardt MT Std by
SJmagic DESIGN SERVICES, India.
Printed and bound in the UK by CPI Group (UK) Ltd.

The Publisher's authorised representative in the EU for product safety is Authorised Rep Compliance Ltd., Ground Floor, 71 Lower Baggot Street, Dublin D02 P593, Ireland.
www.arccompliance.com

For a complete list of Pen & Sword titles please contact
PEN & SWORD BOOKS LIMITED
George House, Units 12 & 13, Beevor Street, Off Pontefract Road,
Barnsley, South Yorkshire, S71 1HN, England
E-mail: enquiries@pen-and-sword.co.uk
Website: www.pen-and-sword.co.uk

or

PEN AND SWORD BOOKS
1950 Lawrence Rd, Havertown, PA 19083, USA
E-mail: uspen-and-sword@casematepublishers.com
Website: www.penandswordbooks.com

MIX
Paper | Supporting responsible forestry
FSC® C013604

Contents

Acknowledgements

My wife, Patti, supports me in every way. Without her cooperation, I could not write this book while promoting my first, RAZOR 03, A NIGHT STALKER'S WARS, and working a day job in Emergency Services. Not only do I love her, but I owe her many thanks.

Friends, Pilots, Flight Engineers, and Medics from the 160th helped me recreate timelines, details, and, in many cases, dialogue. If I couldn't get exact phrasing, I tried to capture the gist of conversations. Remember, this is a memoir, and I focus on the stories from my perspective. "I did this, I did that, etc.", but I always had a crew accompanying me into danger. Without them, I could not have pulled off many wild schemes I dreamt up, and they deserve credit even if it is only in the background for now.

Brigadier General John Dailey, a man who needs his own book, CW4 Juergen Stark (RIP), and Tom Meador gave me insight into the early days of the 160th that I'd never heard, even after serving there for seventeen years. They graciously shared their time with me, as did CW4 Cal Dockery, CW4 Steve Vasek, CW4 Brian Russell, Dan Devine, and one of my favorite flight medics, C.J. Porter.

Pen and Sword Publishing has been fantastic. I'm grateful for another opportunity to share the journey of a Night Stalker from assessment to retirement with some interesting and exciting stories in between. My editor, Chris Evans, supported my efforts in a way that made me want to write more books. Telling stories is fun, and if you've done something you feel is worthy of putting down on paper, I encourage you to do so.

To close out this acknowledgment: This book has been reviewed by the US Department of Defense Office of Prepublication and Security Review (DOPSR) and is cleared to be published as amended. So, in the interest of privacy and OPSEC, I've changed some individuals' and organizations' names, objectives, and target names. The views expressed in this publication are mine and do not necessarily reflect the official policy or position of the Department of Defense or the US government. The public release clearance of this publication does not imply endorsement or factual accuracy of the material. That's a lot of words to say that the Pentagon is okay with me publishing this work. I hope you enjoy my story. Night Stalkers Don't Quit! (NSDQ).

Afghanistan

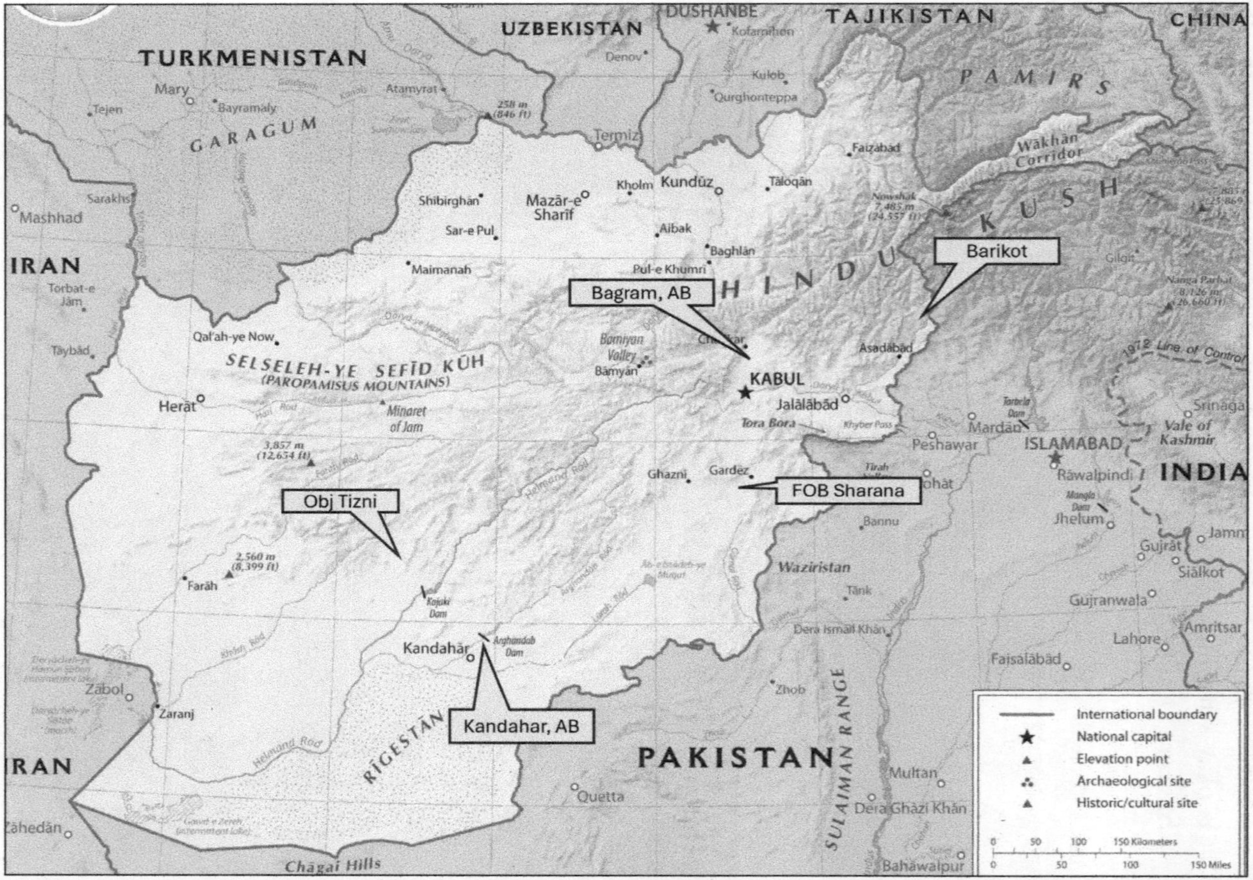

Iraq

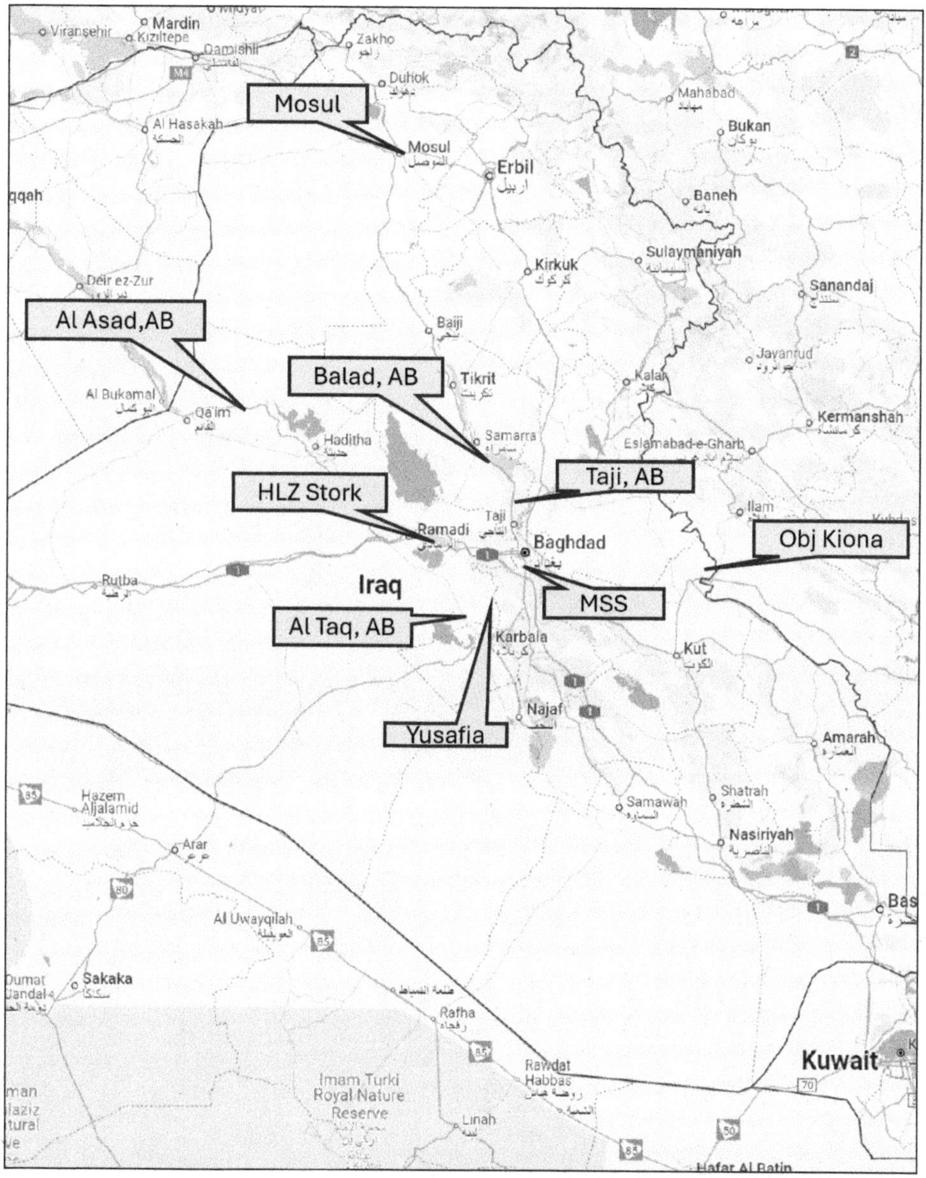
Mosul
Al Asad,AB
Balad, AB
Taji, AB
HLZ Stork
Obj Kiona
MSS
Al Taq, AB
Yusafia
Mardin
Kiziltepe
Viranşehir
Qamishli
Zakho
Duhok
Mahabad
Bukan
Al Hasakah
Erbil
Baneh
Sulaymaniyah
Kirkuk
Sanandaj
Deir ez-Zur
Baiji
Javanrud
Tikrit
Kalar
Kermanshah
Al Bukamal
Qa'im
Haditha
Samarra
Eslamabad-e-Gharb
Ilam
Taji
Ramadi
Baghdad
Rutba
Iraq
Karbala
Kut
Najaf
Amarah
Hazem Aljalamid
Samawah
Shatrah
Arar
Nasiriyah
Al Uwayqilah
Sakaka
Rafha
Kuwait
Rawdat Habbas
Imam Turki Royal Nature Reserve
Linah
Hafar Al Batin

Chapter 1

DUSTWUN

Balad Iraq – May 2007

Humans are more important than hardware, or so I've been told. So, like our high-tech, highly modified Chinooks, I needed to maintain an elevated level of readiness. My physical fitness regimen for the day brought me atop a hardened concrete aircraft shelter baking in the hot Iraqi sun. I was exhausted after only three repetitions in a five-set exercise consisting of uphill sprints and downhill walking recoveries. The steep, sloped concrete was slippery, barely traversable, and the heat emanating from the surface was almost unbearable.

I wanted to continue, but first, I tried to take in the scene – a good excuse to take a short break. As a Night Stalker, I worked from sunset to sunrise as a matter of operational tempo. A daylight view from this elevated position was rare. It was 4:00 pm, nearing the end of the workday for most military and civilians operating at Balad Air Base. Usually, I'd start my day in the climate-controlled gym instead of baking in the 100° heat. But I figured a change of scenery would do me good, and a little sunshine would brighten my day, literally.

Although there were no clouds above, I couldn't see far across the sprawling base due to one irritating restriction to visibility: the ever-constant smoke from the nearby trash burn pits. A lack of wind let the smog-like residue settle over the area like a thick London fog. "This can't be healthy," I said out loud to no one.

My shadow was getting longer as the sun set behind me, and it was almost time to get to work. I glanced at my watch and then down to the airbase ramp to the aircraft parking area.

Five MH-60K Blackhawk helicopters sat idly to my right, ready for the night's mission that was sure to come. Four MH-6 'Little Birds' were forward-staged at our Mission Support Site (MSS) in Baghdad.

My helicopters sat roughly 200 meters to the left in their parking area. Smoke-filled air made it tough to make out the silhouettes of two MH-47E Chinooks.

They're a sight to see if you've not seen one before. Think of a flat-black Greyhound bus with a pointy nose; that'll help you picture the general shape. The 'Forty-Seven' is enormous, roughly 50 feet long and 10 feet wide, allowing a wide range of cargo and passengers. Two three-bladed 60-foot diameter rotors sit on pylons at the front and rear of the top of the airframe. Two turbine engines producing over 4,500 shaft horsepower in normal operating conditions sit externally above the aft cabin area on either side of the aft pylon.

I glanced again at my watch and then back to my Chinooks.

These were two of four MH-47s in Iraq; the others were stationed near the Syrian border at Al Asaad Airbase. Six more Chinooks and their crews operated at various Forward Operating Bases around Afghanistan. But these two were my responsibility. I was the Flight Lead and carried the callsign Sumo Two-Three. My Chalk Two, or second Chinook, was Sumo Two-Four. Our name paid homage to Japanese Sumo Wrestlers – big, strong, and unexpectedly fast.

Major General Stan McCrystal commanded our Joint Special Operations Task Force, and he operated from the same bunker where we planned, briefed, and launched our missions supporting the Global War on Terror. Speaking of whom, I now saw him running behind the tall concrete barriers, conducting his physical fitness routine. I figured I'd better return to my workout before he noticed I was sloughing off.

The walk down the concrete embankment was strenuous on my back and knees, but I had to get to the bottom for another sprint to the top.

"Hey, Al."

Someone was calling my name. "Al, wait. I need to talk to you."

My Officer-in-Charge, or OIC, was trying to get my attention.

The young Captain jogged in my direction and was fully dressed in his flight suit, not PT gear. No workout for him; Captain Sullivan was in a genuine hurry.

"What's up, sir?"

"Al, the Colonel wants to see you in the planning area. He says it's important."

It's too early to need me. Nightly missions don't usually drop until 7:00 PM; something big must be happening, or so I thought.

+++

Lieutenant Colonel Heath Nomi stood among a cluster of planners in the Operations Center: The Black Hawk Flight Lead, the Intelligence Sergeant, the weather forecaster, and a gaggle of Battle Captains.

I took the most direct path before speaking.

"Sir, what have you got for me?"

He handed me a report marked DUSTWUN, with the images of three missing US soldiers from a conventional Army Division. The acronym stands for Duty Status/Whereabouts Unknown.

The young men had been manning a small post just outside of Baghdad near Al Taqa when a large force of enemy insurgents attacked them. An Iraqi and one US soldier died during the assault, leaving the remaining three as abductees.

I read the situation report and looked at my boss. "Sir?"

"Al, these missing guys appear to be in the hands of Al Qaeda in Iraq. We've identified a source that claims to know their location."

"Okay, what do you want from me?"

"Al, we need you to fly to Mosul Airfield to pick up the source and his handlers. Take them to Camp Cropper for interrogation and vetting."

Mosul was way up North, about 170 miles as the crow flies. That's a little over an hour's flight for me. "Why not send a C-130?"

"It'll take too long to get one, and even though a C-130 can land at Mosul and Baghdad International, the handler wants him to go directly to Camp Cropper for Operational Security considerations."

"You'll see when you get to Mosul – The source is overweight. I mean, he's enormous and can barely walk.

"Okay," I said. "It's still daylight; when do you want me to leave?"

"As soon as you can."

"Yes, Sir." I turned to walk away. "How fast do you want me to fly?"

"Burn Rubber," was all he said.

Chinooks are fast. The maximum speed exceeds 190 MPH. However, the actual speed is dependent on the rotor balance and track. The answer I sought was how hard to push my aircraft, and now I knew – *pull out all the stops*.

+++

I alerted my crews and ran to exchange my workout clothes for a flight uniform.

The crew chiefs headed to the helicopters to remove covers, ropes, and chains while the Flight Engineers brought the Auxiliary Power Units (APUs) online.

Twenty-five minutes after receiving orders, I slid into the cockpit and gave a thumbs-up to my copilot, Arthur, already in the right seat. So once I plugged my flight helmet into the Inter-crew Communications System (ICS), I placed the Number One Engine Condition Lever in the Ground Idle position.

I depressed the floor mic switch. "Crossfeed is open. Forward and aft fuel pumps are on. Fuel pressure lights are out."

Arthur nodded in agreement, then quickly noted that he'd already completed the customary radio checks with Chalk Two.

I radioed my second Chinook. "Sumo Two-Four, conduct engine start. "

He replied, "Roger Two-Three, engine start."

I glanced at the overhead panel. "Rotor brake is released. One to start," I announced. My right hand hovered underneath the overhead panel near the engine start switch, waiting for the expected reply.

"Number one is clear to start," my crew chief replied, standing below the left engine.

"One to motor," I said, holding the starter switch to the left. The rotors began a slow rotation in opposite directions. The four Multi-Function Displays (MFDs) were no longer static as my inboard screen showed the engine instruments, and Arthur's displayed the powertrain consisting of five transmissions.

"NG is stable at 49%. Oil pressure is above 5 PSI." I scanned the cockpit and continued. "Good start on one."

"Roger. Good start on One, moving to Number Two," came the intercom reply.

We repeated the process for the right engine and continued with the run-up procedure.

"One and Two to Flight," I announced as I advanced both Engine Condition Levers. The turbines smoothly powered up, spinning the rotors faster and faster until they reached 100% RPM.

The Chinook sounded unique in the helicopter world with its double rotors. In my opinion, no single-rotor aircraft could match its majesty.

My four enlisted crew members moved to their respective stations, raised the ramp, and told me they were ready to conduct hover checks and were prepared to fly.

I looked to my left, right, and overhead before asking Arthur to lift off.

Although the airfield consisted of concrete and asphalt, plenty of sand lay between the two runways and off to the side, where we were situated. Steel planking tied two taxiways together, forming a nice drive-thru parking area for us. But, even with a covering of three-inch river-rounded rocks to keep the dust down, our rotor wash would kick up a hefty cloud.

Arthur already had hover symbology selected on his inboard MFD for the off-chance he lost visual contact with the outside world due to a rotor-induced dust cloud.

Sumo Two-Four reported that they were ready on the Fox Mike (FM) radio.

+++

Thirty minutes after receiving initial orders, we were in the air, headed north.

Arthur accelerated until the Cruise Guide Indicator needle pointed to the top end of the green arc with occasional bounces into the yellow range, indicating that this was as fast as we should go to avoid a condition known as retreating blade stall.

"Okay, gents," I said. "Left Seat is inside. Arthur, you've got flight director guidance direct to checkpoint number fifty-two. Keep your speed up; we're holding steady at 160 knots. You might get another ten out of this beast as we burn off fuel."

My flight engineer, Sergeant Will Baggens, waited for a pause in my flight checks. "Sir, request to test-fire guns."

I raised the red guarded cover, engaged the master arm switch, and looked up from my fuel calculations to verify we were not near any built-up areas. "Clear to test-fire."

Seconds later, the two electric six-barreled Gatling-style M-134s came to life. The minigun, as it's called, is manufactured by Dillon Aero and fires 3,000 rounds of 7.62 by 51 mm. The sound is something unique for a machine gun. Instead of a rat-a-tat-tat like our aft-mounted M-240, the minigun roars like a lion – "BRAAAAAAAAP."

My side window was open, and I could feel the overpressure from the left gun, especially when the gunner traversed forward. The scent of the expended propellant wafted into the cockpit – *This never gets old*, I thought.

The gunners checked in. "Right Gun is operational and cold."

"Left Gun is operational and cold."

"Two-forty is operational."

"Sumo Two-Three, Sumo Two-Four on Fox Mike. All guns operational."

"Roger Two-Four, both aircraft – all guns are up."

I finished my cruise checks and placed a map on my left knee, though I didn't need it to navigate since a digital map now displayed our location on my inboard MFD. A paper chart was handy to mark enemy activity or annotate unlit towers or other unknown hazards to flight.

With my cockpit chores completed, I could now take in the countryside and sights. I found it helpful to get a good look at terrain features and ground texture during daylight to help me in future imagery analysis. *Learning never stops*, I thought just as several tracer rounds climbed toward my cockpit from the left front.

"We're taking fire from eleven o'clock," I said without needing to. Arthur was already maneuvering to avoid the stream of bright green 14.5 MM tracers.

My left gunner immediately returned fire. "Left Gun engaging target ten o'clock low". The minigun roared, and the low-light tracers found their mark, stopping the flow of incoming projectiles. "I think I got 'em, sir."

I marked the location of the enemy gun on my map. You never knew when the enemy would show up. It could be weeks before we get shot at again. I acknowledged his comment and let my wingman know we'd neutralized or maybe destroyed the target, then returned to enjoying the scenery.

+++

Daylight was turning to dusk, making the ground and other hazards more challenging to see. I figured it was time to 'goggle up.' Dusk became night as I slipped a set of Night Vision Goggles onto my helmet and flipped them down. The NVG binoculars sat in front of my eyes about an inch from my face. The luminescent green glow comforted me as it replaced the black of night.

Not long after sunset, I could see the Mosul airport ahead. Arthur had been there before, though I had not. "Arthur, you know where you're going?"

"Yup," he said before angling toward the main parking ramp. "I'm not sure exactly where they want us."

I finished the Before Landing Checklist and radioed LZ control that we were arriving from the south.

Our precious cargo was waiting at the northeast corner of the concrete parking area.

"There", I said. "Look at the light-colored van at one o'clock. It's got an IR strobe on the roof. Land near them."

Arthur set the massive helicopter beside the van just outside our rotor disks, and my crew prepared the aircraft.

"Sir, ramp coming down." After a brief pause, the Right Ramp crew chief drew my attention to the approaching handler and Iraqi source.

Oh my God, I thought. That is the largest human I've ever seen. "Guys, I don't think the source will fit in a seat. Toss a blanket on the floor and throw a 5,000-pound tie-down strap over him. He's huge."

"Sir, you said he was overweight, but he's massive."

"Yeah, how's he doing?"

"Sir, he's walking, or maybe waddling is the best description. Either way, he's not moving very fast. He might have a heart attack before we get him on board."

"All right, let me know when we're ready to go. We have to haul ass to Baghdad. Lives are on the line."

+++

Arthur turned us southbound, running just under 170 knots and 300 feet above the ground (AGL). "Okay, boss, is this altitude good?"

"Yeah, this is fine. You have steering guidance for checkpoint seventy-three. Follow your cues."

I was already thinking ahead.

Once we arrived at BIAP, I'd drop off our passengers at the Camp Cropper helipad and haul ass back to Balad for follow-on guidance, if it came at all. There was no telling if this mountain of Jello held any helpful information regarding the DUSTWUN location. I could only hope – so onward we flew.

The moon had not yet risen, but the cloudless star-speckled sky provided sufficient ambient light for a clear NVG image. And Iraq, unlike Afghanistan, had much more cultural lighting. Sometimes, merely a glow in the distance made the horizon obvious, which helped stave off visual illusions or spatial disorientation. If I had to fly in the Middle East, Iraq was my preferred location. And if my flight that night wasn't so important, I might have relaxed long enough to enjoy the beauty of the stars.

I would typically have steered away from the Tigris River and its populated banks, but I assumed some risk by flying along the heavily vegetated area to save time. The palm groves were an excellent place for enemy troops to hide heavy machine guns or other anti-aircraft artillery (AAA) to ambush unsuspecting helicopters, similar to the attack earlier in the evening on our way to Mosul. I figured that, for the most part, we'd be hard to see. The moon was still not up, and the street lights' glow didn't reach my cruising altitude.

A quick scan of the instruments showed sufficient fuel; all pressures and system temperatures were in the green range. Arthur even managed to eke out a few more knots, and we were now flirting with 170 Knots Indicated Airspeed. A slight tailwind pushed us up to 200 knots.

After several minutes of a quiet cockpit, Arthur broke the silence. "What do you think, Al?"

"About what?"

"Are those guys still alive, and if so, does this asshole know their whereabouts?"

I thought about my answer before speaking. "I just don't know Arthur. I can't discount the fact that he might have valuable information. Every second counts if those missing soldiers are alive, so keep pushing this baby to her limits. The sheet metal mechanics will have a fit when we return. Who knows how many rivets we've popped on this little excursion?"

"Yeah, I guess you're right," he said. "Hopefully, we can find those guys before anything happens to 'em."

"Start a climb to 2,000 feet. I think we can pick up more of a tailwind."

Sure enough, our speed picked up another thirty knots. 230 knots shortened our flight significantly. And as we got closer to BIAP, I felt sick. Had I moved as fast as possible? Would we be in time to save the DUSTWUNs? I wanted to believe the three missing soldiers were still alive as I pushed my fingers deeper into my Nomex flight gloves in nervous anticipation.

+++

Ten minutes from landing at Camp Cropper, I finished my Before Landing Check.

"Systems – NR is 100%, torque is matched, transmission temperatures and pressures are normal." I glanced up briefly to confirm we were descending from our cruise altitude. "Arthur, can you do me a favor and turn on the Aft Fuel Pumps?"

"Roger, Aft Fuel Pumps are on. BIAP runway is in sight."

"Thanks, we're headed for the southwest corner of the airfield. Go ahead and put runway One-Five Right out the left side and fly down the ramp toward the revetments." Although I'd dropped off detainees many times, this passenger was special. I wasn't sure exactly where to go, so I called the Tactical Operations Center (TOC) for confirmation. Colonel Nomi wanted me to land next to a white Hilux pickup truck marked with an infrared strobe light.

"Sumo Two-Four, this is Two-Three. Did you copy where to land for passenger drop off?"

"Roger Two-Three. Do you see the Hilux at one o'clock? It looks like 200 meters ahead."

"Got it; we're beginning our approach." I pointed to my right front; Arthur nodded and began his landing.

Light talc swirled around our aircraft. My window was still ajar, and I could taste the dust – maybe even a little grit in my teeth – a *reminder to myself. Close the window during landings and takeoffs.*

With our brakes set and cargo ramp down, several men assisted the overweight source onto the back of the Hilux pickup truck. As they drove away into the labyrinth of Hesco barriers, I could imagine the struts and springs straining against the load in the bed. My God, that man was enormous. I could only hope he knew where the missing soldiers were. Even if they were already dead, retrieving their bodies was essential to us.

"All right, guys, good job. He's in good hands. Let's get back to Balad. There are likely to be targets developing as we speak. I want to get some chow before the night really kicks off."

The crew was in agreement – time for food.

+++

I reached for my checklist, but it slipped to the cockpit floor just out of my easy reach. Chinook seats have a slight back tilt, making them reasonably comfortable in flight, but this creates a minor inconvenience when climbing into or out of the seated position. Adding body armor with M-4 magazines mounted to the chest and retrieving a dropped item could pose a challenge. So, I loosened my lap belt for an extra inch of reach. I almost had it; my fingers flailed a hairs-width away until I strained a little more. Finally, it was in my grasp. When you think of combat flights, you imagine bullets whizzing by, rockets exploding, near misses, and damaging impacts. Still, it's the little things a pilot worries about – letting a map get sucked out the window, dropping a pencil into the directional pedals, or needing a bathroom break at the most inopportune times.

Enough of cockpit duties; I wanted to wiggle the sticks for a change. "Arthur, do you mind if I fly?"

My copilot was ready for a break. "You have the controls," he said.

I flexed my gloved fingers and lightly gripped the cyclic stick with my right hand. Then I extended my legs so the balls of my feet met the directional pedals, and pulled my helmet mic closer to my mouth with my lips. "Okay, Before Takeoff Check is complete if you guys are ready in the rear."

The crew chiefs chimed in. "Ramp's up, aft ready."

"Forward ready, clear for flight."

Arthur alerted Chalk Two about our pending departure. "Sumo Two-Four, this is Two-Three, pitch-pull in five."

I silently counted to five and lifted the Thrust, known as the collective control, in a single-rotor helicopter with my left hand. The two powerful turbine engines responded immediately with no rotor droop. The talc I thought had blown away lifted back into our rotor wash, creating a circular spark halo along the rotor tip plane.

Once the radar altimeter indicated 10 feet, I applied pressure to my directional pedal, which caused the fifty-foot-long airframe to pivot around its center point. Satisfied that my Night Vision Goggles (NVGs) provided a clear video, I eased the cyclic stick forward to accelerate to 80 knots Indicated Airspeed as we climbed to our cruising altitude of 500 feet above the ground (AGL).

Arthur armed the Missile Warning System. "MWS is Armed/Auto."

The missile countermeasure system would passively monitor for man-portable anti-aircraft missiles. MANPADS lock on to and track an aircraft's turbine engine exhaust, allowing them to home directly at a moving aircraft and hit with a high probability of destruction. The MWS, upon detecting a missile launch, automatically deploys flares designed to mimic the seeker head's target. Although the countermeasure flares can be deployed manually, a missile engagement happens quickly, so the automatic mode is considered the only likely survival option.

Chalk Two was in formation, so I accelerated to our max range airspeed – 138 knots. With our Iraqi source delivered, we were no longer in the same hurry as at the beginning of our flight. But, as I said, no matter how easy the flight, you've got to be wary of unexpected enemy attacks. I say that because if we got too close to an area of Baghdad known as Sadr City, we'd routinely receive accurate anti-aircraft fire from the Shia stronghold.

This night was one of those moments as heavy caliber tracer fire arched across my field of view. The geometric pattern drawn across the sky was beautiful in some strange way, but very deadly. Each flaming bullet had five to seven unlit rounds between them. The 14.5 MM machine gun must have been rocking because the rounds kept coming, and with each fraction of a second, they edged closer to me.

Years ago, as a young pilot, I was taught to break contact with the weapon by banking hard away from the fire and descending as quickly as possible, known as deploying to cover. This briefs well, but any trained gunner can easily anticipate the descent, lead the aim of the evading aircraft, and put steel on target, as they say. Luckily, later in my career, I had the benefit of flying with a British RAF pilot using a radical tactic. He proposed deploying to cover is great if you can immediately place an object, such as a building, hill, or tree, between the aircraft and a gunner. But more than likely, you'll be stuck in open air with the gunner holding the advantage.

So, if you can't defeat the gun, you outsmart the gunner.

I began a slight climb and gentle bank toward the gunfire using his philosophy. I started a silent count in my head – 1, 2, 3, 4, descend. A mere 300 feet per minute drop was imperceptible to the enemy, but now my door gunner could place accurate fire on the point of origin. My crew achieved their second kill for the night as the anti-aircraft fire abruptly stopped.

Chalk Two tried to be helpful but was slow to join the incident. "Sumo Two-Three, you're taking fire from the right."

"Two-Four, thanks for the update – that gun is neutralized." Sarcasm can be fun.

+++

The rest of our flight to Balad was unremarkable; my stress level was much lower with our mission accomplished. I figured we'd land, conduct a quick post-flight inspection, and get food before the usual mission-set began. "Guys, I'm gonna ask to land directly to our pads."

Arthur nodded in agreement as I depressed my cyclic stick mic trigger. "Balad tower, Sumo Two-Three, flight of two, 500 feet, 10 miles from sector Tango, inbound with information 'Mike.' Request landing direct to Sumo Parking."

"Sumo Two-Three flight, Balad Tower, wind calm, clear to land at Sumo Parking, remain this frequency after landing. Revised altimeter 29.83."

"Alright, guys, three minutes out, descending to 300 feet, and slowing to 80 knots. Before Landing check is complete if you're ready in the back."

"Aft ready."

"Forward ready."

After a glance below, I lowered the Thrust and eased back on the Cyclic stick, simultaneously descending and slowing to land. I searched for the windsock to confirm the control tower's estimate. The orange windsock hung limp on its pole. So, I felt no restriction about how I approached the landing area. At about 30 feet, I coordinated the flight controls to swing the rear end of the Chinook to the left, aligning the airframe with the parking pad. There wasn't much of a dust cloud, but you never know; sometimes, the ground is crusted and blows away, revealing a deep talc obscuration. Not this night, totally clear.

Crew calls began at about 15 feet.

"Sir, aft gear is off 10 feet; slide left three – clear down left."

"Clear down Right."

"Aft gear is off five, four, three, two, one, contact. Ground contact lights illuminated."

"Forward gear is still off: two, one, contact."

I neutralized the controls and handed them back to Arthur. "You have the controls."

"I have the controls," he said. Then, we began the laborious process of shutting down.

+++

We hadn't been in the cockpit for long, but I needed to stretch my legs and alleviate the bane of helicopter pilots – back pain – the weight of body armor and several M-4 magazines added to the strain.

My body armor made a thud as I dropped it and sat on the cabin floor to stretch with one leg over the other knee. A little torso twist and a muffled and relieving pop came from my lower back. *Ah, that felt good.*

Staff Sergeant John Hamilton, my Flight Engineer, was evaluating what appeared to be a bullet hole above one of the circular cabin windows. "Hey, Sir, looks like we took a couple of rounds of 14.5mm."

"Oh, how many?"

"Can't say for sure yet. I see three entry holes and can only find one exit." His flashlight swept the floor, sides, and ceiling until he found two spent rounds embedded in wire bundles. "Found 'em. They didn't hit anything critical, but I'll get avionics out here to verify."

I switched legs and twisted my torso in the opposite direction, creating another satisfying pop. "Okay, let me know what they say; this thing needs to be flyable. We have no spare."

"Roger that, Sir."

I thought we got off scot-free with the two Triple-A attacks, but one or both guns poked holes in our sheet metal. But I was confident we'd be back in the fight within the hour if need be. "Hey John, did you put my extra T-shirt somewhere?"

"Yes, Sir. It's behind the right ammo can."

With the Iraqi heat, exchanging a sweat-soaked shirt for a dry one is refreshing and would make the rest of the night more tolerable, especially if we went back out.

I removed my M-9 pistol from its flight holster, slid it into my regular Kydex holster, and stacked my body armor, pistol belt, and map bag in the left cockpit seat. My M-4 rifle remained mounted near my emergency egress door in case we went back out. The race to transport the Iraqi source to Camp Cropper was simple but essential. I was satisfied we'd done our best. Not every mission has to be wild or exciting to be meaningful.

"Hey Arthur, grab your reflective belt, let's get some chow, I'm starving."

Chapter 2

The Storm

Balad Iraq – May 2007

Good food always improved my mood overseas. Most nights, the culinary capabilities of the hairy, beard-net-wearing men made me smile. Chicken wings, chili on rice, or chicken cordon bleu that looked like baked hamsters were the best, or maybe a nice hot slice of SPAM. I'm just kidding. The food was never great, but it was certainly adequate.

My stomach growled as I opened the entryway door to the kitchen.

Captain Sullivan came up from behind. "Hey, Al, the Colonel wants to see you again."

Surely there's time to grab some munchies, I thought.

"Seriously, Al, he wants you now." *Crap, I'm not going to eat tonight.*

+++

Déjà vu. The commander was standing in the same spot as the last time I saw him. His arms were crossed and his brow furrowed. "Al, that fat piece of crap identified the location of the three DUSTWUN soldiers. Chuck Wiley is en route to the MSS (Mission Support Site) with five Blackhawks. I want you to meet him there with your Chinooks as soon as possible."

"Am I moving Fatboy around again?"

"No, you guys are going to the 'X' with as many 'pipe swingers' as you can carry. We're gonna throw everything we have at the bad guys – now get moving."

"Yes, Sir," I said as I headed for aircraft parking. Arthur was right behind me, and by the looks of it, everyone else was already at our two Chinooks. By everybody, I mean my two crews and the maintenance 'Push package,' consisting of a Gator tractor, an Avionics repairer, an aircraft electrician, an Engine repairer, and a Technical Inspector (TI). I loved having the maintenance guys along to fix equipment failures. They were like a traveling NASCAR or Formula One Pit Crew.

Aircraft problems were now the least of my worries, and since they were all smiling, I figured they had fixed damage from the previous flight's bullet impacts.

As I approached, I spun my index finger in a wide circle over my head, representing spinning rotors.

A platoon of Army Rangers filed toward the aircraft as we prepared to start our engines.

We 'cranked' and flew to the MSS as fast as possible. We passed Sadr City, expecting another AAA attack, but none came. I finished the Before Landing Check as we passed Saddam's Victory Arch. The massive crossed swords looked impressive on MFD video as the nose-mounted Forward Looking Infra-Red sensor (FLIR) swept over the structure.

On short final, we passed over the MSS perimeter wall. Only two spots remained in the crowded parking area – we landed and began to shut down. Our rotors coasted to a stop as I looked around to see which rotary-wing platforms we were working with. Four 'Little Birds' sat toward the western edge of the compound with five MH-60s between us and them. We could carry a formidable load of assaulters with this many helos.

"What do you think, Arthur? We got enough airframes for this?"

"Hell yeah. Let's get inside for the brief."

+++

CW5 Chuck Wiley tapped away at his calculator as we entered the cramped and sparse planning area, walls plastered with maps and satellite imagery. He looked up, satisfied that his calculations were correct, and smiled when he saw us.

"Chuck, do you need anything from us?"

He tapped his briefing map. "Yeah, Al, what can you carry to here?"

I took my turn tapping out a performance number on my pocket calculator. "I can carry seventy troops into the objective and ninety out."

He smiled. "Ninety? That's a tight fit, don't you think?"

"You know it is, but you asked. I can carry whatever you can fit in the cargo cabin."

"Cool. That gives us options that I hope we don't need."

"True," was all I said.

+++

With the Air Mission Brief (AMB) complete, I walked down the short staircase onto the dark street and returned to my Chinook. I wasn't sure if my eyes needed to adjust or if it was darker than earlier.

I couldn't see the stars or constellations that dotted the sky during the earlier flights; they were missing. A thin, overcast cloud layer had moved in even though the weather forecaster hadn't mentioned it. He did say a front would move through, but not until sunrise.

Upon reaching my aircraft, I told my crews what we were doing. The mission was straightforward. The two AH-6 attack helicopters would depart first, then reposition to the five and eight o'clock positions covering the entire flight from the rear. The two MH-6 'Little Birds' loaded with four assaulters each would parallel our flight route and loiter near the objective area after we inserted the main assault force. Their role as the Immediate Reaction Force (IRF) was crucial for corralling the target area. If anyone tried to leave, known as 'squirting,' the IRF would intervene and infil their assaulters strategically, thus intercepting any fleeing military-age males (MAMs).

The five MH-60s carried the main effort – eight passengers each. They would Fast Rope into several walled compounds, breach the targeted buildings, and attempt to rescue the DUSTWUN hostages if present.

Our two Chinooks would land on the outer perimeter of the objective, and each would insert thirty Army Rangers as a cordon. Nothing would get past them, in or out.

Once the insertion was complete, we'd return to the MSS and wait for exfil or Casualty Evacuation (CASEVAC). My crew acknowledged the brief, and we waited.

+++

I checked my watch; Wiley was uncharacteristically late for the communications exercise. I could imagine him frantically trying to get his cockpit in order and wanting to get things rolling. A loose packet or a dropped COMSEC fill was the most likely culprit. Then I heard his call on the internal net. "Flight, this is Paladin Six-One on 'Fox Mike, secure, Radio Check.'"

Then, the lengthy but necessary process continued as each aircraft answered in chalk order by airframe type. First, the MH-60s (Paladin), then the MH-6s (Able), the AH-6s (Valiant), and, last but not least, our MH-47s (Sumo).

He then repeated the process on the UHF, VHF, and SATCOM radios.

The process was well-practiced and proceeded without issue.

"Flight, Paladin Six-One, engine start. When ready, give me an 'Eagle Count' and an 'Up' call."

My focus was no longer on the big picture but confined to my helicopter. The other aircraft were smaller and simpler to operate; thus, quicker to start. They'd be ready to fly before me if I didn't hurry. I read my checklist as fast as I could reasonably move without missing a step.

The rhythmic beat of our twin rotors fueled my excitement and anticipation of the action to come. We were heading into one of the most dangerous areas in Iraq – Yusafiah, the last known location of the three missing US soldiers. The only place potentially more hazardous at that time was Fallujah, but I was prepared to meet the enemy on our terms. My thoughts were interrupted by radio traffic.

"Flight, Paladin, Six-One is 'Up' with eight 'Eagles.'

"Paladin, Six-Two is 'Up' with eight 'Eagles.'

"Paladin, Six-Three is 'Up' with eight 'Eagles.'

"Paladin, Six-Four is 'Up' with eight 'Eagles.'

"Paladin, Six-Five is 'Up' with eight 'Eagles and one dog'

"Valient Four-One is 'Up.'

"Valient Four-Two is 'Up."

"Able Seven-One is 'Up' with four 'Eagles.'

"Able Seven-Two is 'Up' with four 'Eagles.'

Finally, it was our turn. "Sumo Two-Three is 'Up' with thirty 'Eagles' and one dog."

"Sumo Two-Four is 'Up' with thirty 'Eagles.'

Wiley now knew everyone was ready and that no other information was required.

"Flight, Six-One, pitch-pull in five seconds."

I've always said that if you can't be at the front of the formation, the next best place is in trail, where you can watch the flight – it's like a movie but real life.

The little MHs struggled to lift their four assaulters over the wall and climb to cruise altitude. The AHs had the same difficulty clearing the obstacles as they clawed their way into the air, loaded with ammunition and rockets.

The Blackhawks had no trouble carrying their load gracefully, climbing out of the MSS, and neither did we.

As we cleared the surrounding obstructions, I twisted the eyepiece focus ring on my NVGs to incrementally improve how I was seeing. "All right, guys, we're ten minutes out. Weapon control status is 'Tight.' Fire at targets positively identified as hostile. Remember that the 'Little Bird Guns' will be to our left and right. Keep in mind not only the impact of fires but also the effects of fires. We don't want to hit our little friends while they're protecting us."

John Hamilton responded on the intercom. "Copy, Sir. Right Gun is Armed and Ready – Tight." The other gunners acknowledged by position as well.

"Arthur, I just finished reviewing the target imagery. Do you want another look?"

"No, I'm good. We'll land with the diamond-shaped building to our right, and Chalk Two will land just behind us and to the left. The Sixties will Fast Rope in several HLZs to our left front."

First impressions of Arthur might lead you to believe his Alabama upbringing was insufficient for the tasks at hand, but he was brilliant with a photographic memory – not a bad pilot either. I noticed he was fumbling in the dark with his intercom radio panel. "Hey Al, I haven't heard anything on the 'Fires' net. Has Wiley checked in with the 'Stack?'"

I reached across the cockpit, pushed his number three ICS pin down, and turned up the volume. He hadn't heard the check-in with the overhead air platforms. The 'Stack,' as it's known, is a who's who of flyable 'Fires' and ISR platforms over the target objective. Wiley checked in with the 'Stack' controller, callsign Darko Zero-Three.

Darko coordinated the pre-assault holding patterns and deconfliction altitudes for all supporting air assets from his specially equipped ISR airplane, ensuring a robust airborne inventory.

I listed the overhead assets for Arthur. "Darko has an AC-130, callsign Hammer Eight-One, orbiting at 10,500 feet; two F-15Es, callsign Dude One-Five and One-Six, are on the tanker and will return in one-five minutes." I paused for a sip of water, then continued. "There are two armed UAVs at 18,000 feet and two A-10s at 15,000 feet, with two more on the way."

Arthur acknowledged, adjusted his helmet, and tightened his chinstrap. We anticipated needing this much firepower to keep our assault force from being overwhelmed by superior enemy numbers. Our guys had the advantage of speed, surprise, and violence of action, but any holdup or delay of our operation would shift the advantage back to the defending enemy force. All would be well if we kept the pressure up and the overhead ordnance falling.

+++

One minute from landing, a 14.5 MM anti-aircraft machine gun opened fire at one of the Blackhawks. The AH-6s began their pre-assault fires run, known as the 'Bump' Maneuver – their timing was as impeccable as their aim. I couldn't see the tiny attack helicopter coming in from behind me. Still, Valiant 41's stream of bullets poured onto that gun to neutralize the operator and serve as an aiming mechanism for the pair of 2.75-inch folding fin rockets that would culminate the gun run. The two AHs completed their break, picking up a low orbit, and waited for another target.

Wiley called for an infrared laser to mark his intended landing area. "Darko Zero-Three, Paladin Six-One, 'sparkle' – on."

From 21,000 feet overhead, an IR laser emitting from Darko terminated at the center point of Wiley's HLZ. "Darko, Paladin, I have visual, 'Sparkle' off."

And just like that, the laser was gone.

I was no longer interested in any other aircraft. We had to put our guys in the correct landing spot among the buildings and compounds. I pointed to our right front. "Arthur, there's the diamond-shaped building."

"Got it, I'm inside on the hover page."

His transition onto his instrumentation was the standard action during a visually obscured landing, which this could be. Lucky for us, the vegetation in the landing zone helped keep the dust down. Arthur put the Chinook where we should be as my crew went into action.

"Ground contact lights are on, ramp coming down – troops unloading – offload complete – ramp is up – Aft Ready."

"Forward ready, cleared for flight."

"Before Takeoff Check is complete, come on up," I said to my crew, and then I announced our takeoff to the flight for airspace deconfliction. "Sumo flight is coming out." There was no visual obstruction, and we could see clearly. "Sumo flight is clear of the dust."

Besides the gun Valiant destroyed, there was no violent opposition to our rotary-wing assault, though the fight would be intense for the 108 men and two dogs we inserted. We returned to the Baghdad MSS to refuel and stand by for potential contingencies or exfil, and, by the way, it was an excellent time to get some food. You never know when things can go sideways, and you get busy. If I've learned nothing in my years of combat deployments, I eat when I can, sleep when the opportunity arises, and most importantly, use the toilet at the first urge to go. At this moment, I did two of those three – sleep was the only one I had no time for.

+++

The MSS was a group of hotel-like buildings once used to house guests, dignitaries, and Saddam's sons. Once plush and vibrant, I'm sure they were something special in the wonderful world of Saddam Hussein, but now they were bomb, smoke, and fire damaged. Bullet holes riddled once immaculate walls, and plywood covered every window.

We repurposed the structures for our use. Special Forces Teams from the Commander's In-extremis Force (CIF) held one building, and we owned another two, including the walled-in courtyard that served as our heliport. The food wasn't bad, although the selections and choices were limited. I spun my fork around my disposable plate, gathering a mouthful of spaghetti and meat sauce as Arthur joined me in the planning area.

"Al, the enlisted guys are fed and hanging out at the helicopters."

My crew was resting, but I wondered where Chalk Two's pilots were. CW4 Steve Vasek and his copilot, CW3 Joe Warner, disappeared when I went to the dining room to get food, and I hadn't seen them since. "Have you seen Vasek?"

Arthur pointed behind me as the two pilots entered the room, carrying a bowl of Baskin-Robbins ice cream.

"Where did you get that?" I asked.

Steve was tall and thin, with an infectious laugh. He always wore the proverbial cat-swallowed-canary smile. "Well," he said, "I suppose if you looked downstairs in the assault force living quarters, you might find a huge freezer full of this tasty frozen delight."

"I didn't know we had that available," I said.

"We don't. The assault force does, and it's not easy to find, but here it is – yum."

CW4 Mel Swearingen was our liaison to the assault force. He came into the planning area with a worried look on his face. "Have you boys been following tonight's operation?"

I occasionally glanced at the televised ISR feeds from the overhead platforms. Still, I hadn't paid close attention since the main objective had been taken in a fierce firefight about an hour earlier.

I finished swallowing a mouthful of spaghetti and told him no.

He was so excited that he spat when he talked. "The weather moved in, and I mean it moved in big time. Look outside; it's raining cats and dogs."

I went to the front entrance, and sure enough, the wind was howling, with huge raindrops falling nearly sideways. "Holy crap, Mel, this was un-forecast. The weather guy said the night would be beautiful."

"I know," he said. "The problem is the stack is gone."

I looked up into the storm. "What do you mean, gone? Surely, someone would stay even in this weather. Our guys are in Yusufiyah; that's a bad place to be outnumbered with no overhead assets."

An un-forecast thunderstorm was terrible, but in this part of Iraq, a collapsing thunderstorm can take things from bad to worse. We'd have to see what happened next. The crappy weather would probably keep your average terrorist undercover, but the hard-core baddies would stay and fight.

I went back into the planning area to find the Air Force weatherman. He was nowhere to be seen. He'd been sent on an errand since the weather was originally so nice. There's a lesson to learn. The weather always has the potential to turn.

Roughly an hour later, Wiley went out to see if the conditions had changed – they had. The rain and wind were gone, but a heavy, thick fog took their place. I knew exactly what happened; no meteorologist was required. The thundering downpour added moisture, especially along the Tigris River, allowing temperature and dewpoint to match or at least get within 4 degrees. The frontal passage produced strong winds, which drove sand and dust particles high into the air, forming condensation nuclei, and then the wind dropped off, leaving a light breeze that provided a mixing action. The result was several thousand feet of thick fog with a solid overcast sky. The aerial fire platforms could return, but wouldn't see the ground through the obscuration. The F-15Es might be able to drop GPS bombs, but that would be risky for the assault force.

+++

Meteorology is a science mixed with art, math, and voodoo. Often, the forecaster is correct in guessing the upcoming weather; sometimes, they are not. Our guys missed the storm and its subsequent aftermath, but it was apparent that the current conditions would stay until well after daylight. Our assault force remained in the most inhospitable location in Iraq with no way out. The fog was too thick for trucks or armored vehicles, and nobody could fly.

Mel came back into the planning area looking for me. "Al, the Task Force Commander wants to see you."

He accompanied me to the Tactical Operations Center (TOC). Colonel Meeler was staring at an Intelligence communications intercept. He spoke when I got closer. "The enemy knows our guys are alone on the battlefield and are attempting to gather a much larger force to take advantage of our situation. We feel the weather will hamper their efforts to mass forces until the sun rises, but then this crap will burn off, and they're likely to overwhelm our guys." He looked up, and we locked eyes. "Mr. Wiley says Blackhawks and Little Birds can't fly. He says they can't go out in this – but he tells me you can. Is this true?"

Wow, this was a big 'ask.' The ceiling and visibility were zero-zero. Wiley was correct; they couldn't fly. Could I? Thanks to our response to 9/11, I was one of Afghanistan's original Task Force Dagger Flight Leads. I'd used the MH-47E's unique capabilities to fly through mountains with this type of visual obscuration and performed our first-ever self-generated approach in a similar zero-zero environment. But there was a fundamental difference. That visually obscured approach and landing was to an airbase runway clear of obstructions and other hazards, making an instrument approach imminently doable.

Standing before him, I felt light-headed as I calculated an estimate of aircraft engine and system performance. The commander stared at me, awaiting an answer I couldn't give, just yet. We could fit and lift the entire force with two MH-47s. Engine power wasn't the issue – it's that we couldn't see to fly. But this is why I was a Flight Lead; I had imagination and determination.

"Yes, sir, I can get your men. I'll need 30 minutes to plan the flight," I said as I turned and walked away. I noted the time – 30 minutes was not long. I first needed a place to land the helicopters, so I called CW4 Scott Wilson, our imagery analyst at Balad. He knew where the original exfil HLZs were. So, there we were, in two geographically separated locations – him at Balad on his high-speed imagery computer and me at the MSS on a laptop, going back and forth on the phone discussing potential approach paths and coordinates. He could see electrical poles and wires and mensurate their height using his high-resolution Geospatial images. Within minutes, he helped me select an area large enough to land two MH-47s with enough buffer space to allow slight drifting upon landing to prevent a collision with nearby obstacles or, worse, each other. I wanted the ground force to send someone to walk the grounds to verify our choices. Once we had confirmation, we solidified the plan.

Steve and Joe double-checked my calculations while Arthur loaded the air checkpoints, flight plan, and HLZ coordinates onto data cards we'd upload into the Chinook Integrated Avionics System (IAS).

The plan was risky but straightforward: My aircraft, Sumo Two-Three, would depart on a magnetic heading of 270 degrees and climb to 1,000 feet, then turn left toward aerial checkpoint thirty-two. At ACP thirty-two, I'd engage a self-generated approach with a glideslope of 4.5 degrees, a speed of 80 knots, a final altitude of 40 feet, and a speed of 0. Once we arrived over our coordinates with zero drift, we'd descend using the hover symbology until landing. We'd use a similar process to climb out of the HLZ and fly back to the MSS. If we couldn't break out of the clouds upon return, the contingency was to fly directly to Balad airbase and execute a standard Instrument Landing System (ILS) approach. Our passengers would remain over day at our facilities instead of the MSS. Sumo Two-Four would depart the MSS using slightly different headings, altitudes, and landing coordinates to deconflict and avoid collision.

After briefing our plan, I nodded to the other Task Force pilots as I headed out the door. Some must have thought us nuts; others may have wished to be us, but we were all Night Stalkers, and we had to be smart enough to know the Chinooks and crews were the only assets that could pull this off – and that was still a maybe.

+++

Darkness and thick fog made looking out the window a joke. There was nothing to see. This flight was like something you'd try in the simulator: A series of simple tasks strung together in a complex scenario.

The Chinook was running with all systems operational. I've done some dangerous and challenging flying in my career, but this was something new, so I dug my fingers deeper into my flight gloves and tapped my heel in nervous anticipation. The digital clock blinked to remind me it was time to go.

I keyed the floor mic. "Sumo Flight, this is Sumo Two-Three. Pitch pull in five seconds."

Arthur was staring at his MFDs and increased power with his left hand. He lined up the velocity vector and acceleration cue for a perfect vertical lift-off. I looked out the front window, then the side window, and finally my chin bubble. I couldn't see a thing, just fog. At 300 feet AGL, Arthur began accelerating to eighty knots with a standard rate climb to our planned altitude; the aircraft could take over once there.

Altitude, speed, and directional cues looked good. "Arthur, I'm going to couple the Flight Director."

He acknowledged as I pressed the coupler button, and the MH-47E again began to earn its pay.

Time at altitude was not going to be long. So, I completed my checks, turned on the window defog, and switched on the wipers. I verified the air-to-air TACAN, which showed Chalk Two's distance behind us – 2 NM. So far, so good. We were both in the air with the briefed separation. "Hey Arthur, we're approaching the 'Top of Descent.'" The TOD is the point in space where the Chinook descends on the pre-programmed glideslope and approach heading.

My heart was pounding; This was exciting, stimulating, and scary all at the same time. I had to keep my wits. Too many people were counting on us to make this work. I supervised the Flight Director's commands and monitored aircraft movements closely in case I needed to intervene manually and fly the approach. None of us could see outside, so I called out our progress to the crew. "Guys, we are descending on glideslope at 800 feet per minute; our speed is seventy-five knots and slowing. Altitude is 400 AGL – looking good."

"Sir, we're ready in the rear."

"Thanks, guys. We're at 40 knots and 100 AGL – looking good, but I still can't see the ground. The radar is clear, with no obstacles to the front." I looked at Arthur; he was glued to his instruments, as he should be.

The Voice Warning System (VWS), known as 'Bitchin' Betty,' spoke to us. Her digital voice was as irritating as ever – "Warning, Altitude Low, Altitude Low." Arthur acknowledged her with a tap of his thumb as we came to a hover, visually obscured.

"40 feet, 0 knots – no drift – looking good. Alright, coming down," I said as I entered zero in the control data unit by my right knee.

Arthur aligned the approach cues, and we touched down at our intended HLZ.

"Longitudinal Cyclic Trims are at ground, clear to lower the ramp," I said.

"Ramp is coming down; assault force is approaching us from five o'clock."

I looked out every window I could access and still could not see beyond our rotor tips.

Chalk Two was on the ground within two minutes of our touchdown. Everything was still going to plan. Now, we had to take off with a full load and hope the enemy hadn't figured out what we were up to.

I sequenced our flight plan to the next checkpoint and waited for the troops to finish loading. It would be a squeeze for the passengers. Remember, we put them in using five Black Hawks and two Chinooks, and were now utilizing only the two 'Forty-Sevens' to bring them home.

Chalk Two's radio call broke my daze. "Sumo Two-Four is 'UP' with forty-three eagles and one dog."

I reciprocated. "Sumo Two-Three is 'UP' with sixty-five eagles and one dog; Pitch-pull in five seconds."

Arthur repeated a similar ritual to the one he used to begin this nutty experiment: getting into the air. Within a few minutes, we found ourselves over the top of the MSS at 1,000 feet, looking down through the clouds. The fog was clearing enough that I could see well enough to land.

"Arthur, I've got the landing area in sight and have the controls – coming left and down, guys. I'll orbit in a descent with left turns and land in our normal spot."

The crew was ready. Sumo Two-Four followed our actions, and with a gentle flair, I touched down softly, followed by Chalk Two. *My God, we did it*, I thought.

+++

If we hurried, we could still return our Chinooks to Balad in the dark. I didn't want to fly over Baghdad in daylight hours if I didn't have to, fog or no fog. *Why tempt fate?*

It'd been a long duty period, starting with the flight to Mosul to retrieve the DUSTWUN source. The objective had been a 'dry hole.' No Americans were onsite. We did find some valuable intel for potential follow-on operations and passed it on to the conventional forces. This night was a lot of work for very little return, but we had to treat every mission as if someone's life depended on it, because if it weren't someone else, it would be our lives. That's why Night Stalkers Don't Quit.

+++

Sunrise was now an hour behind us as I crawled slowly up the side of my Chinook back at Balad, checking for post-flight damage and performing a pre-flight inspection for the next flight. While atop the helicopter, I took the time to survey the airfield as I often did. The sun was rising quickly, and thanks to the night's rainy weather, the burn pit was not throwing the typical lung-biting smoke plume across the runways. I couldn't believe we'd pulled off the exfil. Few people thought we could, but quality training, experience, proficiency, and a fantastic helicopter made the seemingly impossible task possible.

General McChrystal was waiting to congratulate us. Then we ate, showered, went to sleep, and repeated the process again and again.

Our actions to retrieve the assault force deserved a reward. The next night at the MSS, the Task Force Commander thanked me and offered to let us share their ice cream.

I didn't have the heart to tell him we'd already been raiding his stash. He wouldn't have cared, but it would have diminished his thankful offer. We brought his men home when others wouldn't or could not – this wouldn't be the last time…

Chapter 3

The Night Stalkers

The Organization

Fielding the CH-47 helicopter in 1962 enabled the US Army to modernize its movement of troops and equipment on and around the battlefield in Vietnam. The tandem rotor design of the CH-47A and B brought capabilities and performance not previously possible in Army Aviation. Ten years later, newer materials, technology, and innovation improved the airframe, evolving into the CH-47C. The 'Charlie' was nearing the end of its service life when the 1979 Iranian revolution resulted in 52 US Embassy personnel taken hostage.

The subsequent rescue attempt, Operation Eagle Claw, was designed around a rotary-wing assault force carrying Special Operations Forces. CH-47Cs were the helicopter of choice, but for OPSEC purposes, the helicopters selected were Navy RH-53s flown by US Marines. The choice was easy for planners; after all, Army pilots didn't fly from Navy ships, and Chinooks didn't have shipboard capabilities such as folding rotor blades.

The mission failed during its first refueling stop in Iran, known as 'Desert One.' Although there were planning mistakes, equipment, and training limitations, the predominant factor was an unforecast sandstorm and follow-on fog.

President Carter publicly acknowledged the failure and accepted responsibility. He also authorized a second attempt: Operation Honey Badger.

Planners for the new operation would benefit from hindsight and lessons learned.

SF would remain the assault force; however, the rotary-wing element was wholly revamped into a task force created from conventional units around the Army and Army National Guard. The soldiers trained to operate from Navy ships, fly in adverse desert environments, and fly in the dark with Night Vision Goggles (NVG). They became so proficient at night operations that they gained the nickname Night Stalkers.

But when the Iranian government released the hostages in 1980, leaving no reason to execute another military incursion into Iran, the units involved in Honey Badger melted back into their regular duties. The Night Stalkers, however, would not return to their original units; instead, they formed a permanent organization that morphed into what would eventually become the 160th Special Operations Aviation Regiment in October 1981.

The 160th SOAR grew into three battalions: The First and Second Battalions call Fort Campbell, KY, home. The Third Battalion resides at Fort Stewart's Hunter Army Airfield, and the Fourth operates from Joint Base Lewis-McChord near Seattle.

+++

The 160th's aircraft each have a niche and individual mission. All crews can perform crossover missions, though specific airframes may be better suited for certain environmental conditions, desired speed, or flight distance. For example, only a 'Little Bird' can land on the bridge wing of an embarked ship, fly to an austere airstrip inside a C-130 airplane, or land on a moving train.

The armed Blackhawks (DAPS) rival their AH-6 brothers in rocket or gun accuracy, but they can fly faster, higher, and refuel in the air, giving them some distinct advantages.

Chinooks and the slick MH-60s have the most similar missions – long-range infil/exfil and assault, to name two. There are many more that I'll talk about as I continue this story, but before I share more missions, I want to mention that the modified black helicopters that make up the fleet are not the reason the Night Stalkers are so successful; it's the people. You heard me say it before: Humans are more important than hardware.

As a human, I've got a disclaimer. Although this book is mainly told from my perspective, I was never alone during my easiest or most daring and dangerous flights. I had a copilot, an enlisted crew of four to six crew chiefs, often a medic, and occasionally an air mission commander on board. Oh, and don't forget I usually had one to ten helicopters flying in formation behind or alongside me. In addition to the aircrews, the support team was crucial. Our fuelers, maintainers, staff members, and intel folks may be the best in the Army, maybe even the entire military.

Acquiring special helicopters and the tools needed to penetrate enemy nations' defenses isn't easy, but the Regiment's Systems Integration and Maintenance Office (SIMO) makes that happen.

What's the saying? "If it were easy, anyone could do it." The special operations community is usually called into action if a situation is complicated or of national significance, where failure is not an option. So, how does the United States Special Operations Command (USASOC) attract, select, and hold on to soldiers of the desired caliber, skills, experience, and mentality?

Joining the Regiment is voluntary. Pilots will not be directly assigned and must volunteer. Enlisted soldiers can volunteer, but may also be sent directly to the unit. However, the entry-level training will weed out non-performers or soldiers who don't want to become Special Operators.

I want to serve with people who want to be there. I don't want a 'ticket puncher,' nor do I want some adrenaline junkie who just wants to do cool stuff. Here are my thoughts on selection as an evaluator and instructor pilot; I will limit this discussion to a Chinook pilot's experience.

Of all the volunteer applications our recruiters receive, roughly 25% are rejected outright, and another small percentage is eliminated after a closer review. Eligible pilots are invited to Fort Campbell to show their skills and try out.

Assessment week involves a physical fitness test, a psychological evaluation, and a general aviation knowledge test. Before flying in the Regiment's helicopters, a flight simulator period will familiarize the candidate with the cockpit layout for safety purposes. It's also a chance to demonstrate features that make some special operations easier and, in some cases, possible. When conducting an assessment, I viewed the candidate as an ill-informed equal.

Because the 160th is somewhat secretive, pilots in the conventional Army don't understand what we do or how we do it. Some are closed-minded about our organization and think we're a bunch of 'cowboys' flying around with our hair on fire, performing the most unsafe acts. They believe we throw aviation regulations out the window and don't follow any rules. The truth is that we have a different set of rules. Assessment is about finding pilots who are willing and able to adhere to them.

+++

CW2 Calvin Dockery thought he was being punctual when he walked into the Fort Campbell Combat Mission Simulator (CMS) building thirty minutes early. As a member of the 101st, he flew CH-47Ds in the first months of Operation Enduring Freedom. We'd crossed paths in the mountains of Afghanistan, but didn't know it then, though we would soon enough.

As the evaluator, I arrived for my scheduled simulator period and sat in an empty briefing room. I must have waited fifteen minutes before I realized no one was coming to meet me. I shivered and noticed the cold air conditioning for the first time. Irritated, I looked at my watch. Where was my candidate? I searched the offices, the bathroom, and the hallways before noticing the MH-47E bay was active. The full-motion simulator stood 30 feet high on hydraulic legs, providing pitch, yaw, and roll motions to replicate flight movement. On the outside, the 'box,' as it's known, looked like a medium-sized shipping container. But inside was a mock-up of an MH-47E cockpit. There was no need to look elsewhere. He had to be in there.

I walked across the enormous, well-lit bay toward the console phone. I was angry that Calvin hadn't waited for me, and I intended to let him know once I climbed the ladder to the cockpit, which was descending by now. Air pressure relief valves opened with a hiss as hydraulic actuators locked in place, so I could safely climb the ladder.

I secured the security rail at the top of the ladder and entered the 'box.'

I exchanged pleasantries with Steve, the console operator, then turned my attention to the man in the left seat. He looked about 5′10″ with a medium build and red hair; not just any red, but fiery red. "CW2 Calvin Dockery?" I asked.

His polite manner and genuine smile were the first qualities I noticed as he stuck out his hand. "Yes, Sir, you can call me Cal."

I began to smile, then stopped myself. This is how civilized gentlemen introduce themselves, but for now, this is an evaluation; we're not meeting over a warm cup of hot cocoa with marshmallow bits. I needed to regain the evaluator vs. candidate dynamic. For the next week, we could not be friends. "Cal, were you not told to wait for me in the briefing room?"

"Yes, Sir, but…"

I cut him off abruptly. "I don't know what army you're in, but the one I'm familiar with, we follow instructions." I felt a little guilty as I applied pressure. "Maybe we should just end this evaluation right now. You obviously don't want to be here; otherwise, you wouldn't sit in my seat."

Cal looked around, rethinking his surroundings and placement. "Oh shoot, I'm sorry, Mr. Mack." He locked eyes with Steve; his body language and eyes pleaded for help, though none came. Steve hadn't screwed him on purpose, but he wasn't going to help him either.

"Cal, get out of my seat so we can get this over with."

He nervously unbuckled his harness and shifted to the other side of the cockpit. He had energy, and though stressed, he was ready to go before me.

"Mr. Mack, I apologize for getting off on the wrong foot with you."

"Cal? Don't suck up, it's unbecoming." I unpaused the machine, and hydraulic actuators lifted the simulator to its full height. Realistic video panels replicated windows, making for an accurate flying simulation. "Cal, I want you to pick up the helicopter to a 10-foot hover, perform a VMC takeoff with a right-hand traffic pattern, and land back to this very spot".

He followed my instructions with very smooth and well-executed maneuvers. My attempt to rattle him had no effect. I looked across the cockpit and could tell he couldn't help himself; he wore a huge smile – he was enjoying this. I'd never seen this during an assessment. Most guys are so nervous that they fumble, stutter, or present such a severe, overwhelming look that I must try to lighten the mood to gauge their personality – not with Cal.

"Alright, you can fly; let me show you some of the 'toys,' meaning the special mission equipment." I took the time to explain the cockpit setup and how the old 'Delta' Model steam gauges he was used to were replaced with four Multi-function Displays, known as MFDs. "Cal, each MFD can display any information you need. If needed, we can fly this aircraft with only one of the four and maintain full functionality, even if slightly inconvenient." I pointed at the old-style Attitude Indicator, Altimeter, compass, and turn and trim indicator. "These standby instruments will work well enough to get us home in a pinch."

Cal just soaked up the entire conversation.

"The flight controls are the same as what you're used to, although the cyclic grip is slightly different – notice the shape and buttons."

He looked around. "There's way more than the 'Delta' for sure. What's this thumb button near the top?"

He was pointing to the Voice Warning System or VWS. "That button will wear out your flight glove. It's how we silence 'Bitchin' Betty.' She's the computerized voice that warns or advises you about things you should know.

"What does she say?"

"I want you to take off, and I'll demonstrate. Go up to 300 feet AGL, 100 knots Indicated, and heading 360 degrees." Then I changed my mind. "I have the controls. I'm going to fly."

"Roger," he said. "You have the controls."

I climbed into the simulated air and sped up. "Okay, Cal, you see that data pad by your left knee? Use the alphanumeric keypad to change our low altitude alert to 350 feet AGL."

After analyzing the data screen, he changed the value, and Betty started alerting. Her computerized voice cut through any cockpit conversation, even with her starting tone, which was at an average volume. "Warning—Altitude Low—Altitude Low." I ignored her, and she got louder and more obnoxious. "WARNING—ALTITUDE LOW—*ALTITUDE LOW.*"

"There are two ways to shut her up." I exaggerated my thumb movement on the cyclic stick. "You can acknowledge her by pressing the ACK button or correcting the condition." I increased power with my left hand; as we climbed above the pre-set altitude, she reset and waited for our next alert. "Here's what you'll hear the most". I raised the Thrust control toward my armpit until the power indicator, measured in torque, exceeded 95%.

Betty chimed in immediately. "*Torque – Torque – Torque.*"

Cal was suitably impressed, so I showed him a capability I knew he'd never seen before.

First, I needed the console operator to replace the cartoonish visuals with the TOPSCENE Database and change our location. "Steve, can you put us south of Kabul at 500 feet AGL?"

The visuals paused as we were transported just east of an extensive mountain range about 5 nautical miles south of a sprawling Central Asian city. "This is Kabul, Cal." I pointed out key landmarks, and Cal noticed an unexploded bomb on a small knoll and pointed it out.

What we could see was a hyper-accurate simulation using authentic one-meter imagery.

"Cal, I didn't realize you flew around here. Were you at Bagram?"

"Yeah, I was there during the 101st initial deployment and flew in Operation Anaconda like you."

If I thought I liked him before, I knew it now. "Look to your left. Do you see that small compound with the American Flag?" I told him the story of flying the CENTCOM Commander and his entourage to the embassy in 2001 and being fired at by two MANPADs. Countermeasures decoyed the heat-seeking man-portable missiles as I delivered General Tommy Franks to the opening ceremony. "Check this out. We're gonna land inside the compound with loss-of-visual conditions – this is called a 'Bravo' approach."

Cal was silent as I explained the setup and maneuver.

I picked up a 300 feet-left orbit to evaluate the wind strength and direction. "It looks like the wind is coming from the northwest at about 5 knots. We'll make our approach facing that direction. I will use a steeper-than-normal VMC approach to the ground and coordinate my altitude and speed as I descend along my intended angle." I continually adjusted my speed to be half my altitude and called it out over the ICS. "I'm at 80 feet and 40 knots – Hover Page is available." I pointed to the MFD, which displayed our current velocity, direction, and trending ground track. "See this forward-facing line? I will keep it to our front and eventually bring it to the center crosshairs as we slow below 10 knots." I paused for a long moment as a dust cloud engulfed the helicopter. With only the instrumentation, I needed to align all the desired parameters. "40 feet and 20 knots – 20 feet and 10 knots." As the aft landing gear touched the ground, I pitched the aircraft nose up ever-slightly until we slowed sufficiently to lower the forward gear to the ground and applied the brakes. "There, not too shabby, eh?"

Once again, Cal was appropriately impressed. He still had to perform a Navigation flight evaluation and interview, but I felt we would accept him without a problem. With his attitude and skills, I'd see him again in two days, but for now, I had another candidate to evaluate. His recruiting application looked similar to Cal's but had more flight experience and an Instructor Pilot (IP) designation. He had plenty of CH-47D flight time and a suitable amount of night flying, which is always an important skill when you fly Chinooks in the dark.

+++

CW2 John O'Grady confidently walked into the briefing room wearing a sage green one-piece flight suit. Like Cal, he had a head full of red hair, cropped short and neat. But unlike Cal, his was more muted with a tinge of brown. Although his build and coloring were similar to the previous candidate, John wasn't impressed by me – he wasn't even sure he wanted to be a Night Stalker.

Mr. O'Grady was not the least bit intimidated by our selection process. In fact, he somewhat subscribed to the common misconception that special operators are wild cowboys taking unnecessary risks just to be cool, and he said so during our get-to-know-you phase of his evaluation.

Still, there was something about him that I couldn't put my finger on. He didn't seem to fit the mold for guys we'd take. He was skeptical and maybe even somewhat cynical. I could fail him right then and there with no simulator eval. No – I needed to see what he could do in the cockpit. So, after the mandatory maneuvers, I took him to the simulated embassy in Kabul and attempted to demonstrate the same loss-of-visual-reference approach into the walled compound.

I hadn't completed an orbit when John made a comment that brought my blood to a boil. "Mr. Mack, I don't see any reason to proceed with an approach that ends in the dust." He paused for effect – he was instructing me in conventional wisdom: Safety was paramount. "If you can't see out the windshield, there's too much danger and risk. I tell my pilots to go around – after all, go-arounds are free. You guys…

He was talking down to me, so I cut him off before terminating the ride. He didn't know it, but I'd recently returned from a nasty overseas deployment with several close calls, daring rescues, and CASEVACS. I led missions into hot landing zones, saving the lives of several friendly forces and putting my aircraft and crew in danger to successfully bring near-lifeless soldiers home alive to their families. "Alright, you sanctimonious know-it-all, here's the scenario: there's a firefight at the embassy, and one of the soldiers has been shot in the femoral artery. The medic on the ground confirms that if he does not get immediate treatment, he will die on site."

John quietly took in the scene.

"Now – we are going into the embassy compound to exfil the fallen soldier. We know it's dusty on the LZ, and the enemy is still spraying heavy-caliber machine guns to attempt to penetrate the clay walls." I took a breath and got madder. "We have the skills, training, and equipment to save that man's life, and I can do it on the first approach. But if I follow your advice, I should go around at the first sign of dust. Upon climbing out and setting up for another attempt, the enemy knows I'm coming back, and the HLZ is now fouled with my dusty rotor wash.

"That soldier will die with us in sight.

"His family will not celebrate his recovery, but instead will mourn his loss and wonder if anything could have been done." My anger was evident. "Well, Mr. O'Grady, what do you think? Is it worth the risk to our helicopter to save that man's life with a loss-of-visual-reference approach?"

A meek "yes" was all he could muster – he knew he was done.

Or was he?

I took the simulator off-motion and politely asked him to step into the briefing room. I was uncharacteristically flustered, had lost my professional demeanor, and needed to regroup before debriefing CW2 O'Grady.

I returned from the pantry with two chilled water bottles and handed him one as a conciliatory gesture. "Look, John, I'm sorry I laid into you. Something drew you to us. You can see what we are capable of, and I know you want to make a difference. You're good enough to be here. All I ask is for you to open your mind to what is possible when you are well-resourced and trained to fly the most sophisticated helicopters in the world. If you can do that, you'll thrive here, becoming a valuable asset in the global war on terror."

He grinned. "I can do this job; I know I can."

+++

Both men fared well in the remaining selection process. Ironically, I was their primary instructor during Green Platoon and was privileged to serve many years with both. Unfortunately, John died bravely during a risky flight in Afghanistan chasing Mullah Omar, the Taliban leader. You'll hear more about Cal later in this book.

Chapter 4

So you want to be a Night Stalker?

2003

The military response to the attacks of 9/11 in Afghanistan had a high cost in airframes. Task Force Sword, operating from the Afloat Forward Support Base (AFSB) USS *Kitty Hawk*, put four MH-47Es in the hangar for a prolonged repair period. Their bullet holes and environmental damage started a shortage of Chinooks for the 160th. Early in 2002, Task Force Dagger added three helicopters to the list – two severely damaged by RPG and machine gun fire, and one brought down atop Takur Ghar. All but one, aircraft tail number 475, were recovered, rebuilt, and returned to service.

The 160th's second battalion, based at Fort Campbell, Kentucky, initially fielded twenty-four MH-47Es. The prototype, tail number 267, was owned and operated by the Systems Integration and Maintenance Office, known by the acronym SIMO, and was reserved for testing new hardware and software in the continuously evolving world of technology. MH-47E tail number 465 tragically crashed, losing all hands as a result of an equipment failure during a training accident in 1996; another Chinook was lost during combat operations in the Philippines while supporting Operation Enduring Freedom – Philippines (OEF-P).

If the Global War on Terror ended shortly after the initial assaults of 2001 and 2002, the scarcity of special operations helicopters would be inconvenient but not crippling. Unfortunately, not only did the war not end, but America invaded Iraq in 2003 and conducted other special operations around the globe. With Chinooks in high demand, there was a need to return the damaged airframes to service and replace aircrew members lost in shootdowns and crashes.

In the special operations community, there is a list of five tenets named the SOF Truths, which are considered irrefutable.

1. **Humans are more important than hardware.** People – not equipment – make the critical difference. The right people, highly trained and working as a team, will accomplish the mission with the available equipment. On the other hand, the best equipment in the world cannot compensate for a lack of the right people.
2. **Quality is better than Quantity.** A small number of people, carefully selected, well-trained, and well-led, are preferable to larger numbers of troops, some of whom may not be up to the task.
3. **Special Operations Forces cannot be mass-produced.** It takes years to train operational units to the level of proficiency needed to accomplish difficult and specialized SOF missions. Intense training – both in SOF schools and units – is required to integrate competent individuals into fully capable units. This process cannot be hastened without degrading ultimate capability.
4. **Competent Special Operations Forces cannot be created after emergencies occur.** Creation of competent, fully mission-capable units takes time. Employment of fully capable special operations capability on short notice requires highly trained and constantly available SOF units in peacetime.
5. **Most Special Operations require non-SOF assistance.** The operational effectiveness of our deployed forces cannot be and never has been, achieved without being enabled by our joint service partners. The support of Air Force, Army, Marine, and Navy engineers, technicians, intelligence analysts, and numerous other professionals contributing to SOF has substantially increased our capabilities and effectiveness worldwide.

SOF Truths, as listed by USSOCOM

Worldwide deployments were picking up steam, not settling down. We would have to ramp up assessment, selection, and training to get new crews in the field. The question on every Night Stalker's mind was how we could do that without violating the intent of the SOF Truths.

Recruiting was easy. We had an abundance of quality candidates. Many had several hundred NVG hours, a valuable skill for a unit that flies mostly at night. 'Little Bird' and Blackhawk pilots were in less demand due to the extremes of Afghanistan's elevations and distances – Chinook pilots were the hot commodity. So, if finding volunteers is not an issue, then what is? Answer: There were no helicopters to train with. Assessment navigation evaluations needed to be conducted in MH-6s, and the other skills and attributes would be accomplished in the flight simulator. Training with actual Chinooks was going to be a challenge.

Once selected, all Night Stalkers learned and practiced basic skills like combat shooting, advanced first aid, swimming, and dunker qualifications. Enlisted crews and support staff conducted land navigation while pilots moved on to Basic Air Navigation, known as BNAV. This particular phase is the baseline for all Night Stalker pilots. They learned how to create NVG navigation routes and produce flight products, like maps, time-distance-heading cards, and other packet materials. The flight products were essential for in-flight success, but they still needed an Air Mission Brief (AMB) before taking to the air.

Instructors presented techniques for briefing missions, which the students subsequently performed each night. AMBs used informational posters with HLZ diagrams, medical locations, communications, aircraft tail, and crew assignments.

Students navigated to one of many unlit grass airfields in the Kentucky–Tennessee area at night using only a hand-held map, clock, and compass. Their instructor pilot flew the MH-6 'Little Bird'; however, Speed, heading, wind corrections, hazard avoidance, and target identification were the sole responsibilities of the student. BNAV culminated in a final check-ride to one of the more difficult airfields to find in the area, usually in Missouri or Alabama. Timing is essential as each Air Checkpoint (ACP) has to be correctly identified and passed over within two minutes of the planned time.

The ultimate objective standard is finding the landing area and touching down within plus or minus thirty seconds of the scheduled ETA. The reward for passing the evaluation is flying back to Fort Campbell with the evaluator navigating – no more stress.

+++

The next progression for pilots is BMQ training.

Aircraft-specific training starts in the flight simulator and moves to the helicopters for primary flight training. It is followed by special mission tasks like infil/exfil techniques, Terrain Following Radar (TF), Air Refueling (HAR), Desert/Mountain, overwater, and Navy deck landing qualifications. Usually, it is a six- to eight-month process. Shortages of MH-47s to train with were a massive problem. It was time to get creative.

+++

The first twelve-man MH-47 class was about to start in Green Platoon – history in the making. Every one of the students ultimately became a successful Night Stalker. But here's the rub: we would train them with only three MH-47Es. So, we took a lesson from the Army's schoolhouse at Fort Rucker and separated the twelve pilots into two sections: AM and PM.

One IP was pulled from Alpha Company, Second Battalion; two IPs came from Bravo Company. The Special Operations Training Company (SOATC) provided two civilian mission instructors (CMIs), and the Second Battalion Commander loaned me to the team. As the Battalion Standardization Instructor Pilot (SIP), I would ensure that the SOF Truths would not be violated, even with the large student load and shortage of Chinooks.

Each Instructor Pilot (IP) was responsible for two students. My two were sharp. Heck, they were all impressive. The other instructors and I didn't see the inconvenience of the large class as a problem; just the opposite, we were having fun.

+++

160th selection and assessment are designed to bring in skilled pilots with compatible personalities. We needed a personal chemistry that you'd think would be hard to find, but it's not. Professional, hard-working, fun-loving, and daring people are the norm in the 160th – the twelve-man class was full of them. We had two former MH-47 Flight Engineers returning to the unit as pilots: a maintenance pilot, two former Rangers, a former Navy Submariner, and a Navy SEAL who made a bold interservice transfer to attend flight school and assess for our unit. By the way, I found an appropriate nickname for our frogman. I named him 'Otter,' a seal-like creature, and to my joy, it stuck.

So, with our students and IPs assembled, I briefed the class on what to expect: Early days for the morning section and late afternoons for the

PM guys. Day flights were no problem as we began basic flight maneuvers and traffic patterns. A typical training day for the AM section would start at 6:00 AM. The students would gather and request an official Air Force weather briefing. A student would research the Notices To Airmen (NOTAM) and distribute the day's flight packet.

In the meantime, the IPs discussed flight maneuvers to be performed, which students were having difficulty, and which ones were catching on fast. Sometimes, we'd swap students as a quality check or a way to reach a troubled student. Sometimes, a simple instructor change could make all the difference in teaching a variation in technique.

Every briefing begins with a time hack. You've heard it in the old military movies, action movies, or maybe an elaborate heist: "In thirty seconds, it will be 06:30 Sierra." Twenty seconds would pass as the pilots fumbled with their wristwatches to adjust the time so that at the final second's countdown, everyone's timepieces would match the US Naval Observatory Master Clock. "In ten seconds, it will be 06:30 Sierra – five, four, three, two, one, Hack – 06:30 Sierra."

A student presents the observed and forecasted weather for our training area. Then, I explain our training goals for the day, introduce the maneuvers we'll be covering, and confirm which maneuvers they should now be able to perform to standard.

Each day, the class would answer five questions: Aviation general knowledge, aeromedical factors, aircraft emergency procedures, 160th Standard Operating Procedures (SOP), and aircraft systems or meteorology. I'd choose one student to answer each question randomly, and then the IPs had thirty minutes of 'table talk' to discuss whatever they wanted before aircraft tail numbers were assigned. These conversations were valuable in ascertaining our students' mindset and knowledge level before flying. Once completed, we gathered our gear and headed to the flight line.

I saw our assigned Chinook sitting on row three, spot two of the Second Battalion parking ramp. The crew chiefs removed covers and opened panels so we could see what was behind them and verify everything was correct before flying. My students, 'Otter' and 'Sassy,' walked alongside me as we conducted the pre-flight inspection. Along with looking for flaws, I used the opportunity to play 'What's it?' I would point at an aircraft component and ask: "What is it, and what does it do? If they answered incorrectly, I'd give a detailed description and purpose before moving on to the following item. If they got it right, the pre-flight went much quicker. The better prepared they were, the faster we got in the air for the fun parts.

+++

Day flights were straightforward. We'd conduct 'contact' maneuvers such as takeoffs, traffic patterns, VMC approaches, slopes, two-wheel taxi, and simulated engine failures, ending in roll-on landings. Once the students were proficient, we'd move to nights and fly our Chinooks in the dark. Two weeks were enough to gain confidence in operating the enormous aircraft with basic flight tasks.

Next, we'd return to the simulator and practice Instrument (IFR) flying before doing the same thing in the National Airspace.

By now, the guys could safely fly in Day, Night, and Instrument conditions. It was time to add terrain flight, confined areas, and sling loads, followed by Fast Rope, hoist, and aerial gunnery. I want to note that at this stage of the training program, the students are still having fun, but it gets a bit tougher with the addition of special mission tasks like HAR and TF.

Helicopter Air Refueling, like the other tasks, begins in the flight simulator to understand how to rendezvous with an MC-130 tanker in the air and how to take gas in flight. It's not difficult, but it can be more challenging due to rough environmental conditions. Once they get the hang of day operations, we transition to night.

To get qualified, each student must demonstrate proficiency in both pilot seats, the right and again in the more difficult left. But HAR training doesn't stop there; we schedule Marine and Air Force tankers throughout the course to help maintain currency and increase proficiency.

The Terrain Following Radar segment sometimes comes before Air Refueling if external assets are unavailable, but it mostly comes after.

The MH-47E and its replacement, the 47G, have a precious tool for flying in visually inclement weather. The Multi-Mode Radar (MMR) can display precipitation and terrain presence using the weather or ground mapping mode. TA, or Terrain Avoidance, shows the pilots the terrain ahead that is above and in the way of the projected flight path, but the most valuable mode is Terrain Following. The user-selectable clearance altitudes of 100, 300, or 500 feet allow a system-generated cue to command the pilot to increase or decrease the Chinook's climb or descent to maintain the set clearance altitude (CALT).

Using the MMR, pilots can fly over terrain in mountain passes or over the top of peaks without being able to see outside the aircraft. Light rain, snow, fog, and dust are no match for the radar, and it is one of the main success stories of the global war on terror. The first infil missions of TF Dagger shortly after 9/11 were only possible because of this equipment. Conventional Chinooks do not possess an air refueling probe, large fuel tanks, or the MMR, limiting their capability in long-range or adverse conditions. Night Stalkers are the sole worldwide operators of this hardware.

+++

All training flights include a mission management component involving route changes, degraded navigation, simulated equipment failures, emergency procedures, and other flight contingencies. Fuel calculations include how far I can fly, where I can go if my planned fuel is not available, and, always crucial, how long I can loiter before I need fuel.

Our twelve-man class departed for Houston, Texas, to conduct overwater navigation and flight techniques, Helocast, and deck training with the US Navy. Houston has several advantages: It's close to the Gulf of Mexico. There is a nearby air refueling unit with plenty of planes available for HAR over water, and the city has FAA-approved helicopter routes allowing us to fly our Chinooks around the city low-level, during the day, and in the dark.

Usually, we'd finish and return to Fort Campbell for a quick reset, but the time available with our three Chinooks meant we were keeping the line units from using their aircraft. We needed to press on to ensure the helicopters' timely return to their owners.

+++

Albuquerque, New Mexico, provided mountains and a desert landing environment suitable for our needs. We began by flying to our customary training area – LZ Dust. A wide-open valley with salt flats and occasional mesquite scrub was just what we needed. It was dusty but forgiving.

We flew roughly 900 miles non-stop utilizing HAR and arrived at Kirtland AFB around 02:00 AM. Our LOGOPS NCO was waiting at the airfield with our hotel room keys and rental cars. We closed our FAA flight plan, put the aircraft to bed, and proceeded to our lodging for an after-action review and eventual sleep.

Day one of environmental training involves no flying, just setup. The enlisted crews took the opportunity to give the Chinooks a little extra tender-loving care. This trip was an anomaly because the overwater phase usually occurs last, so mechanics at Fort Campbell could properly wash the aircraft. The salt air and water in and around Houston were corrosive to the Chinooks. So, our crew chiefs needed to perform a thorough soap and water wash before we added dust, sand, and rocks to the mix.

The pilots were busy, too, and they used the opportunity to transform a hotel conference room into a planning and briefing area for eventual operations. Our hotel was very generous, providing the space at no additional cost, and management allowed the pilots to move furniture around to suit their needs. Once they rearranged the room, they added poster easels, a computer network, and a laser printer. Of course, in typical Night Stalker fashion, they needed a cross-cut shredder to eliminate their mistakes – considering their level of knowledge, there'd be many.

Around 5:00 PM, I stopped in to check on the students' progress. I was impressed. They'd done a fantastic job, and I told them. "Hey guys, I'm here to check how the setup is going. Do you need anything?"

'Otter' spoke up. "Nope. We've got everything we need. As you can see, the laptops are networked, and we just tested the printer. We're good to go."

"You guys did well; why don't you get some dinner? We'll do a local area brief tonight around 8:00 PM."

'Sassy' had a question. "Al, before we go to dinner, we want to know how well the hover page really works in the dust."

"Well, guys, it works great. But great is relative. When the velocity vector and acceleration cue are over the center crosshairs, you still have about a three-foot drift radius." I paused long enough to sip coffee before continuing. "Considering the airframe is roughly 50 feet long and 10 feet wide, that drift isn't too bad if you're trying to land in the dust to a relatively flat open area."

I had everyone's attention.

"Look, the purpose of training out here is to hover, land, and take off in a visually obscured environment. You guys trained in the simulator, which is a pretty good replication of what you'll experience here, but now we can apply what you learned in actual conditions." I paused again to sip my now-cooling coffee. "Let me tell you a short story about my first experience with the IAS Hover Page. In 1996, I was new to the unit on my first trip as a BMQ. The Echo Models were brand new, maybe a year old. Engineers and Instructor Pilots described how some of this magic equipment works, but everyone was skeptical. Back then, nobody wanted to be the first to transition inside and commit to the symbology." I looked around the room – I still had their attention.

"We were in Georgia conducting bilateral training with the Rangers, and I was in the right seat heading north toward our target, a large dam. CW5 Don 'The Dragon' Tarbon was the pilot-in-command (PIC). He tucked his map under his thigh as we neared the target objective. Back then, there were no lasers to point at the HLZ, but I'd memorized where to Fast Rope my forty-five 'customers' onto the dam, identified it, and began an aggressive approach."

While describing the scene to the students, I unconsciously used my hands to display aircraft approach and attitude adjustments in a typical aviator fashion. "It was a dark night with no moon or stars visible, nor any manmade ambient light to help with the NVGs. I had a lot of goggle time, but this was challenging. The Rangers slid down the ropes from the front cabin door and the cargo ramp, which put me out over the water with the dam and any visual references just behind me and out of my field of view." I craned my neck as far back to my right as possible to demonstrate my predicament.

"I couldn't hold a stable hover. Don yelled at me to hold the helicopter steady so the Rangers could finish roping, but I started drifting with nothing to look at, and the crew chiefs let me know."

"Sir, you're drifting right; come back 2 feet. Roping in progress. You're coming up; come down 3 feet. Now you're drifting left; come back 2 feet."

"Someone was going to get hurt if I didn't settle down. Then it hit me – that hover page was right before me. The velocity vector was moving spastically around the crosshairs, indicating my poor hovering skills, so I focused my attention there, slowing down my cyclic movements. The crew chief became calm as I now held a solid position and altitude. That damn

Hover Page worked great, but only when I finally committed to it. So, I'm telling you that what we're about to teach you guys is a fantastic tool that you will use, especially in Afghanistan."

The students seemed satisfied and ate dinner before our classes and briefing before turning in for the night.

+++

'Sassy' released the brakes and lifted our Chinook to 10 feet as I ran through the checklist items before departing: "Flight Controls – Check."

With the challenge issued, the crew response would be to answer or parrot my calls.

"Flight controls feel good."

"Ground contact lights – Off."

The crew chief at the ramp checked the little press-to-test lights. "Ground contact lights are off."

'Flight instruments – Check." I scanned the instrument panel. All four MFDs correctly indicated aircraft attitude and power used, as represented by torque, engine and transmission temperatures, etc. "Okay, they're good," I said. "Systems are good, AFCS, set to number one, AFCS to number two, and back to both." I compared my performance planning card (PPC) predicted hover calculation to the torque gauge – 60%. "We're good to go."

'Sassy' called for the Before Takeoff Check, which I did, and he departed to the south toward the aptly named HLZ Dust. Once we completed the Cruise Check, I assumed the controls and my instructional tone. "As I scan near and out to the horizon, I'm looking for vertical hazards like antennas and powerlines. If there's vertical development such as hills, upsloping terrain, or ridgelines, always try to leave yourself an 'out' in case you need to turn around or lack the engine power to clear an obstacle or terrain." Before banking to the right and ascending a long parallel ridgeline, I announced my intentions to the crew and waited for the response before turning. No response came, so I repeated myself – still no acknowledgment from the enlisted crew.

Usually, the coordination between the front seats and the back seaters was flawless and almost poetic, or sing-song with the back-and-forth communications, but with students, this was clunky and inefficient. The guys in the back were new to this kind of flying and weren't sure when to speak up. That would change soon. Staff Sergeant Smith tapped the right gunner on the helmet with a three-cell Maglite flashlight to get his attention. "Jones, what the hell – Mr. Mack told you he was turning – answer him".

"Clear right, Sir."

Bitching Betty let me know I was too low for her comfort; *"altitude low, altitude low, altitude low."*

"'Sassy,' reset the VWS to 50 feet."

"Set, 50 feet," was his reply.

I felt like a snow skier descending a rolling slope with graceful slalom turns over gentle moguls and dips. Just then, we crossed the highest elevation in the area, and the whole valley floor opened up before us. No matter how often I fly out west, the beauty takes my breath away when I see it. It was time to have some fun and demonstrate tactical desert flying. "Gentlemen, coming down hard left." I didn't wait for the crew as I dumped the power and turned hard left with a bank angle of 50 degrees.

This time, what the gunners were supposed to say was apparent. "Clear left and down."

As I neared the bottom of the slope, I eased in the power so I didn't mush through and smash into the valley floor. "Clear right – coming right."

"You're clear, right, Sir."

"Guys, you can forget about adding 'Sir.' There's no time for pleasantries at this altitude and speed." I sped up to 140 knots and hugged the terrain to my left and then to my right. The students caught on to the coordination requirements.

"'Sassy,' take the controls and fly. You've got Flight Director Guidance to HLZ Dust. Fly this thing like I've been doing."

"I have the controls," he said, and off we went. He knew what he was doing and had a natural talent for flying. My cheeks hurt from smiling; the day was going great.

The sun was high overhead, and no clouds were in the sky. While 'Sassy' was flying, I took the opportunity to readjust my seat and harness. I tightened my flight helmet with a gentle tug of the chin strap and noticed a smudge on my smoked visor. Luckily, it was toward my cheek, and I could slide my handkerchief up underneath the dark plexiglass to remove the offending blemish before I took a sip of water. Now, I was ready to teach the most challenging part of our curriculum, ATM Task 2130, VMC Approach with Loss of Visual Reference.

+++

Our first landing in the Albuquerque desert was uninspiring, to say the least. The salt flat that composed HLZ Dust was dry, hard, and crusted – this would not do…

"Okay, gentlemen, obviously, we didn't churn up any dust. I've seen more dust come from a water spout on the Atlantic Ocean, but that's okay; I know how to fix that. I have the controls."

'Sassy' looked at me like I was nuts when I began to two-wheel taxi around the landing area, breaking up the surface crust. "Al, what are you doing? You'll make it more dusty and harder to land."

I smiled as I drove around, balancing on the aft two landing gear. If you watched us from outside the helicopter, it would look like we were 'popping wheelies.' "That's okay, guys; we need lots of dust for you to get anything out of this training. It'll take a while, but by the end of today, you won't see anything outside the helicopter below about 80 feet. Trust me, I've done this once or twice."

The sandy grit in my teeth and the coating of dust in my cockpit indicated I might have crunched up enough surface cover to reveal the tan talc-like sand previously covered by the darker salt crust – it was time to have some fun.

I began with some basics. "The first thing to notice is the direction and speed of the wind. Always use it to your advantage. Land, take off, and hover facing into it whenever possible. If you can't, that's okay, but understand how it will affect you." I performed my pre-takeoff checks. "Guys, Left Seat is inside on the Hover Page – coming up to a stationary 20-foot hover."

The crew was ready, and I lifted off using only the Hover Symbology to maintain my height above the ground and my lateral position. "What can you guys see outside?"

I knew the answer, but wanted total acknowledgment from the crew.

Sassy could only see a roiling dark brown cloud of dust, and each crew chief saw the same. However, if they looked straight down, they could see the ground and, to some extent, determine altitude and lateral drift. I knew this was indeed an uncomfortable situation for them.

"Guys, I'm going to execute a 360-degree pedal-turn and return to this heading and altitude – Nose left –Tail Right."

They couldn't see but answered in the only way they knew:

"Nose clear left."

"Tail clear, right."

I completed the turn and demonstrated how to get out of the dust safely before handing the controls back to 'Sassy,' as it was his turn to practice what I'd taught. While he was practicing, the other two Chinooks joined us, and we performed multiple landings and takeoffs until dusk. The next day, we brought along sub sandwiches for dinner. We repeated the previous day's activities until dusk, landed on a nearby ridgeline, shut down, and ate our dinner perched atop the highest terrain in the area to watch a beautiful sunset. Once night fell, we flew our Chinooks in the dark and repeated the day's tasks.

A few nights later, we included mountain flight routes using the MMR for Terrain Following and rendezvoused with a tanker to conduct air refueling in the mountains. We also had an excellent opportunity to test our new supplemental oxygen setup. Instead of an O_2 console with an oxygen mask, each crew member had a cylinder of aviator's O_2 with a nasal cannula. I doubted there would be enough oxygen, but even flying for two hours at altitudes exceeding 14,000 feet, my pulse oximeter showed 97% O_2 saturation, which is my usual reading. It worked fine, and the cannula was more comfortable and didn't block my vision like a conventional aviator's mask – I was sold.

+++

After a week in the desert, it was time to go home, but the return flight would be no walk in the park for the students. The several-hour flight back to Fort Campbell would include their end-of-course test and the BMQ evaluation. Each student would navigate at night to two unlit dirt or grass-covered airfields along the way home. Much like the BNAV evaluation in Green Platoon, one target objective would require degraded navigation, primarily using a clock, compass, and paper map while answering questions about aircraft systems, emergency procedures, SOP, and FAA airspace. After arriving at the first target plus or minus thirty seconds, we'd restore all their systems, and the flight would take a different tone.

The focus on the second leg would involve mission changes and questions about how fast I could get to the target and how long I could hold and loiter before heading to my destination. Where can I divert if we exceed our time and have insufficient fuel? They'd need to demonstrate a working knowledge of the Integrated Avionics System (IAS) by avoiding a reported simulated threat system and still arriving at their target objective, plus or minus thirty seconds, the Night Stalker standard.

All twelve students passed and earned the 160th Basic Mission Qualified Pilot (BMQ) rating. They could now serve as co-pilots with a Fully Mission Qualified (FMQ) Pilot-In-Command. These men would now be assigned to a line company in the 2nd Battalion and deploy to Afghanistan shortly. I knew we hadn't violated the SOF Truths, and these men were ready.

Chapter 5

Afghanistan – GWOT

October 2003

Transportation to Afghanistan can be as easy as riding as a passenger in a C-17 cargo airplane carrying an MH-47. Sometimes, personnel movements don't coincide with a Chinook swap, but I still need to get to Bagram, Afghanistan. We call these trips 'Planes, Trains, and Automobiles,' aptly named after the comedy movie of the same name. In October 2003, I led several new pilots and crew chiefs halfway around the world for our 120-day deployment. The men we would relieve were rooting for us to make seamless connections and fly like the wind, which, from my experience, was unlikely.

Ten of us packed into two fifteen-passenger vans headed for the Nashville Airport. Our biggest challenge would be traveling with our weapons – ten M-4 rifles and a matching set of M-9 pistols were in individual locked gun cases. In addition, I carried a kit bag loaded with a memory foam mattress, a sleeping bag, a 'woobie,' a pillow, a small bath rug, and an electric heating pad. My body armor, plates, and flight gear all fit in another bag, while a large gym bag with a shoulder strap added uniform items for the journey. Of course, my trusty three-day ruck held anything of personal value, not to mention an extra set of underclothes, gym shorts, and a t-shirt. You never know when you'll spend the night without your big bags.

After several trips back and forth from Afghanistan, I'd perfected my packing and selected the exact bags to be able to move the entire load myself in one lift. Each bag was marked prominently with my name and unit because, inevitably, something would get lost, left behind, or loaded onto the wrong plane, truck, or pallet. In over ten years of wartime traveling, I never lost anything for long.

This journey from Nashville to Baltimore was only the beginning. Once in Baltimore, we had to kill time and wait for our late-night departure to Germany. This plane, known as the rotator, wasn't just loaded with warfighters. Families were joining their servicemember spouses serving European assignments, which is not bad; I spent three and a half years in Mannheim, Germany, with my family in the 1980s, but I digress.

I tried to sleep during our long transatlantic flight because I knew the next stage would be mentally exhausting, as this was as far as our plan took us with any precision. From here on out, we were on our own to find transport into the Afghan theater of war.

Upon arrival at Rhein-Mein Air Force Base, we boarded a shiny blue bus to a holding area. I spoke with the airman whose job was to move folks like us along or provide lodging until we could. The young E-4 appeared tired and, I'm sure, overworked. Troops were flowing through this hub and its companion base, Ramstein, to funnel troops and equipment to Operation Enduring Freedom in Afghanistan and the newly opened Operation Iraqi Freedom in Iraq, the latter taking precedence.

After storing our weapons at the armory, we arrived at an old Air Force Barracks. Rhein-Mein Airbase was once the premier facility in all of NATO, but it was heading for the scrap heap as a base. The organizations that once occupied these barracks were long gone. I'd often stayed in this building in the 1990s, waiting for the movement to or from Kuwait during Operations Desert Thunder and Desert Fox. The familiar surroundings comforted me, and I slept soundly until our personal services airman woke me with good news. "Sir, I've got a flight for you to Kyrgyzstan, but you must get your guys to the terminal in thirty minutes. I've got the bus out front."

Considering the short timeline, the guys didn't complain; they packed their gear, boarded the bus, drew our weapons from the armory, and loaded a C-17 bound for Manas Airbase, but we didn't go anywhere. A maintenance problem forced us to unload, turn in our weapons, return to our lodging, and wait for the next day's flight. If patience is a virtue, I was losing mine as we repeated the process twice before taking to the air.

Eventually, we ended up at Manas Air Base Transit Center, but our luck there was no better than at Rhein-Main. We just had no priority in the Air Force system. The face of the Air Mobility Command was usually an Airman or maybe an occasional Sergeant with a clipboard. If you weren't on it, forget going anywhere. I needed to find the officer in charge or a senior non-commissioned officer to kickstart our priority.

A young Major listened to my request for transport into the war zone as he tapped away so fast on his computer that I thought the friction might catch his keyboard on fire. He looked up, smiled, and removed a priority transport request from his printer. "This will get you out of here today. I hope it's what you want," he said.

"Yes, Sir, that'll do. Thank you."

I don't know why it was so difficult to get into Afghanistan, because it was always easy to get out.

+++

We were welcomed with open arms at Bagram. The men we replaced had our bunk spaces ready, our maps marked, and our flight packets printed, cut, and laminated.

Dave, the outgoing Flight Lead, showed me my new desk in the planning area. There were six loaded M-4 magazines neatly stacked beside four pistol magazines. "Here, he said, you're going to need these. Oh, and here is your Blood Chit and Fentanyl lollypop. Don't lose it; they're more accountable than the bullets."

"What time does your flight leave?" I asked.

"Customs inspection in two hours, C-17 loads in four."

This Relief-in-Place (RIP) wouldn't be much of a turnover. I'd already done three deployments to Bagram and one to Kandahar, so I just needed an introduction to the intel officer and our Customers.

Operation Iraqi Freedom was in full swing, with the Operators from Fort Bragg handling the majority of Special Operations in Baghdad, Tikrit, and Mosul. At the same time, a small contingent of SEALS manned Al Asaad airbase out west. The rest of the SEALS kept Afghanistan missions humming along with a Company or two of Army Rangers. One of the downsides to fighting two wars at once is a lack of fires and overhead intel assets – there weren't enough for all the special operations task forces to share equally. Iraq took the preponderance of enablers, forcing us in Afghanistan to either scale back our intel collection or slow down our mission pace. We weren't going to do either; instead, we needed to get creative with fires and ISR. You know the saying, "Where there's a will, there's a way."

I worked my way toward the Intel office, known as a SCIF. I could discuss targeting information and analyze satellite imagery and communications intercepts in the Sensitive Compartmented Intelligence Facility. Every

High-Value Target (HVT) we hit would begin in this room. So, getting to know the Intel, communications, and imagery analysts was an essential first step in each of my deployments.

The SCIF was staffed twenty-four hours a day and run by a young NCO; I'll call him Sergeant Steve, and he was as knowledgeable as anyone I'd met regarding the threats in Afghanistan. I sat quietly, listening to the tall Texan as he discussed the current target set he and the SEALS were working on. South of Kabul in Logar and a little more to the west in Wardak, some Taliban commanders were wreaking havoc with International Relief organizations trying to help Afghans in need of medical care, food, infrastructure repair, and schools. The one thing the Taliban hates more than the US is an educated citizenry, especially girls.

Steve listed two of our top HVTs: Objectives, Scallop, and Salmon. Oh, and by the way, if a bad guy gets a codename, he's probably an HVT or at least an MVT, and he's likely to earn a nighttime visit from us and our pipe-swinging friends, the Navy SEALS.

Objective Scallop ordered attacks in Ghazni, and Salmon was attempting to kidnap aid workers in Wardak. The two communicated regularly, revealing their plans, movements, and timing. I won't discuss how sources and methods work due to classification issues, but you've probably seen enough movies to figure out how we knew what the HVTs were up to.

At this point in the Global War on Terror, special operations missions generally incorporated a deliberate planning process, usually involving days, vs. a hastier timeline involving hours or minutes, known as a Time-Sensitive Target (TST). The plan to go after Scallop and Salmon spanned three days before we finalized a plan using five MH-47Es to transport an assault force of 125 SEALS and Rangers to the 'X.'

Objective Scallop was the furthest away from our base in Bagram, but the elevation was lower and more accessible with less severe vertical terrain, so we'd hit him first, then strike Salmon during the following period of darkness (POD).

I showed my route planner a general flight path I preferred to avoid cultural lighting, built-up areas, lines of communication, and suspected early-warning locations. He came up with the aerial checkpoints needed to form the en route phase of the flight. I also selected the Release Point (RP), which would set a landing direction most aligned with our HLZs. The route planner was also responsible for fuel calculation and performance planning. Simple math could make or break the entire mission, like how much gas we need to get where we are going and how long we can hold and execute an emergency exfil or CASEVAC. Fuel was one commodity we could not do without. If we couldn't carry what we needed, we had to know where, when, and how much we could get later in the mission.

My planning cell XO would keep things on track when I was with the assault force, aka our customers. He still needed to consolidate information such as medical facilities and their capacities in the case of CASEVAC or a mass casualty evacuation. Communication crypto fills had to be coordinated so we could talk via secure radio during the mission.

The Maintenance Test Pilot visited the cell frequently to see what we thought. How many aircraft did we require, and which special mission equipment could we go without if we ran into parts and supply problems? Sometimes, the helicopters in Iraq competed with us for parts availability, and they had priority for at least another year. We'd make do, but sometimes, there'd be a fight for radars and aircraft survivability equipment (ASE). Both theaters of war had dust storms, fog, and seasonal rain, so the MMR was a highly sought-after commodity. I thought Afghanistan, with its mountains, should always win over the plains of Iraq, but I was biased based on my location.

Luckily, all five MH-47s were fully mission-capable, and the maintenance flow chart showed plenty of flyable hours remaining.

+++

Satellite imagery in 2003 wasn't what it is today. The resolution for most of our space-based systems provided ten-meter imagery of the entire region. One meter or finer resolution was only available for the highest-priority targets, leaving us comparing topographic map terrain to grainy shots taken several years earlier – archaic by today's standards but usable.

I sat down with our SEAL planners to select HLZs. Both objectives needed five landing areas for the assault: one planned CASEVAC HLZ and two alternates. I wanted flat-open areas measuring 120 feet wide by 200 feet long at a minimum. In a less dusty environment, we could use something smaller, but these dimensions would be as small as I would plan for this area of Afghanistan. 'Plan' is the key word because, during mission execution, the SEALS would ultimately convince me to land in tighter confines. It wouldn't take much for me to try something daring with my helicopter; they just had to ask.

We agreed upon our landing areas, but I still had much to figure out using another military acronym, METT-T, which represented mission and commander's intent, enemy situation, time available vs. needed, terrain/weather, and troops, equipment, and support assets available – so with mission and intent established, timing synchronized, and assets allocated, what was left to worry about? Afghan weather patterns in the Fall can be challenging to forecast. In this particular autumn, the so-called 120 days of wind lasted well into October – an annoyance but not unmanageable.

Well, we'd deal with whatever conditions we encountered, whether man-made or natural. Our training, experience, and even SOF culture would serve us well if a mission didn't go according to plan. There was nothing left to do but 'get after it.' So, with all our pre-mission tasks complete, we took to the air.

I finished my cruise checks, test-fired the guns, and settled into my usual flight routine, verifying that the flight management software (IAS) calculations matched my Time Distance Heading Card (TDH). I keyed my SATCOM radio to update our Command at Bagram on our progress. "Yukon Zero-One, this is Maxim Two-One. Flight of five, passing ACP number six. All guns are operational; update ETA to 01:10 Zulu – advise all players."

"Maxim Two-One, Yukon Zero-One, copy all."

I refolded my map in anticipation of our next navigable turn and scanned through all my windows, up, down, side-to-side, and, of course, out the front – it was damn dark. The moon had set earlier in the day, but I didn't see any stars, and even with the city of Kabul to my left, there didn't seem to be any cultural lighting. Was there a power outage? That was possible but unlikely. I flipped the switch for the infrared searchlight.

"Dust,' I said under my breath.

The visibility decreased due to suspended dust and sand blowing into the air.

"Maxim Two-Four, can you see me, okay?"

"Two-One, Two-Four, we can see you, but it's getting more difficult to make out your movements."

"Roger Two-Four, let me know if it gets any worse; we may need to separate the flight. Break – Maxim Flight. I'm up Two-One Yankee on the TACAN. Confirm you're receiving it. Respond in Chalk order."

"Maxim Two-Two, receiving TACAN."

"Maxim Two-Three."

"Maxim Two-Four."

"Maxim Two-Five."

Satisfied that the pilots behind me were aware of worsening flight conditions and ready to act, I lifted my water bottle, but it never reached my lips.

My copilot, Rich, got my attention. "Al, I can't see anything outside. I'm holding our altitude and following the course guidance."

"Copy. I'm activating TF with Clearance Altitude – 300 feet. Follow your cues while I sort the flight."

"Roger, Al. Guys, Right Seat is inside and on the TF Cue."

The crew chiefs acknowledged and settled in for a bit of adventure.

We could fly through the mountains using the Multi-Mode Radar (MMR), but I had four more Chinooks behind me doing their best not to collide with each other or the mountainous terrain to either side and above us.

"Maxim Flight, this is Two-One on Fox Mike." I paused a beat and took a cleansing breath to ensure I sounded calm and professional, announcing the brevity code for 'I can't see anything:' "'Blind Alley.' Maintain course guidance with TF CALT – 300 ft. We'll pick up separation using speed differential. I'm accelerating to 130 knots – Two-Two maintain 120 – Two-Three, slow down to 110 – Two-Four use 100, and Two-Five hold 90."

The Tactical Navigation System, or TACAN, could display the distance between two aircraft by selecting a paired channel. I maintained Air-To-Air Channel 21 Yankee, and the other pilots used Channel 84.

The idea in this situation was to get everybody 2 nautical miles apart while still heading along our planned course. Next, I calculated a time to an ACP short of the Objective area that would allow us to rejoin if we encountered suitable visibility. If not, we'd abort and return to base separately.

"Maxim Flight, this is Two-One on Fox Mike; continue with TF active and keep a minimum distance of two miles. Expect a holding rejoin at ACP Twenty – right-hand turns – 80 knots airspeed – 7,000 feet MSL. My ETA is 00:12 Zulu."

Each Pilot-In-Command (PIC) acknowledged and then set their flight management system arrival at checkpoint number twenty, two minutes later than the Chinook in front of them, thus guaranteeing we wouldn't run up on each other.

Success and failure were on my mind. It would be nice to reach the target as a flight of five and capture or kill the HVT. It dawned on me that two of the five copilots were from the twelve-man Green Platoon class, and this was their first combat deployment. Aborting the mission was simple: turn to the east and intercept a standard flight route back to base – the enemy would be no wiser that we'd attempted to hit him. Failure was losing a helicopter and crew to terrain and weather. Each Echo model Chinook costs roughly 50 million dollars; more importantly, each machine carries at least six crew and twenty-five assaulters – one hell of a cost to lose one.

"Rich, how are ya doing over there?"

My co-pilot was calm but focused as he followed the TF cue on the MFD. "Al, I'm good. For all the wind, you'd think there'd be more turbulence in this valley, but it's manageable".

"Cool, Two-Two is running two-point one miles behind us. And we're about to cross checkpoint seventeen." As I crossed it, I restarted my digital clock. Each of the other pilots behind me reported passing over the same geographic point, and I compared it to the elapsed time. If each aircraft was two minutes apart, we maintained a precise separation. The call doubled as an 'I'm still here' notification. If someone failed to check in, I could assume they are no longer in the air and narrow the search area to the last time they checked in.

We were all still on track, and the storm seemed to be easing up. Through the diminishing obscuration, I could make out the ridgelines to the east.

"Rich, I think we're gonna be okay with visibility; it's clearing up. Expect a holding rejoin in about fifteen minutes."

"You got it."

As predicted, I could see at least 10 miles, maybe more. As long as all the aircraft were still on course and on time, we could rendezvous and continue our mission together.

I was nervous as Rich slowed to 80 knots and banked the aircraft to the right at 3 degrees per second. We were now heading opposite the other aircraft, so I turned on the IR searchlight, illuminating our nose. This made it easier for the approaching helicopters to pick us out of the background clutter and, hopefully, reduced the possibility of a collision.

"Right Gun has Chalk Two in sight at three o'clock – they're turning to join."

"Copy; let me know when his IR light is off."

Each pilot-in-command would extinguish their searchlight in reverse chalk order once joined and in formation. Once the pilot to my rear turned his light off, I knew the aircraft behind him was also in formation, and I could turn back on the original course, which we did. I selected the recommended ground speed from the Flight Management System, which indicated that 130 knots would make up our lost time to the Release Point for Objective Scallop.

"Maxim Two-One, This is Frodo with information – prepare to copy."

Damn, I forgot about the airborne intelligence platform. What could he want?

I keyed my floor mic. "Go ahead, Frodo; Maxim is ready to copy."

"Maxim, radio intercept vicinity of ACP Twenty indicates you've been detected by enemy early warning, and your location has been passed by push-to-talk relay in the general direction of your target – Over."

I discussed the possibility of compromise with the assault commander, and he asked me to continue the mission. I wanted to ask for communications jamming, but those assets were tied up in Iraq. We may have lost the element of surprise, so we'd now rely on speed and violence of action.

"Frodo, Maxim copies all."

+++

The Release Point was just around the bend in a small creek we were paralleling. Once we crossed the RP, Rich would slow us to 80 knots and aim toward our HLZ. Each aircraft had a specific spot to land.

"Ten minutes," I announced, and received the usual acknowledgments from my crew.

"Ten minutes – Aft Ready."

"Ten minutes – Forward Ready."

"Just a reminder," I said, "weapon control status is Tight." The gunners would only shoot if we got shot at first – we couldn't initiate an engagement, but we could undoubtedly end it. My crew chiefs were well-trained and ready to rock.

Rich was flying low, hugging the military crest of the ridgeline to our right. The four pilots-in-command behind us tightened the formation as we crossed the RP. We had just under five miles to go, and I pushed my fingers deeper into my flight gloves – nervous energy needed to be released, and I felt the urge to pee, so I tapped my right heel repeatedly and pulled my microphone closer to my lips to compensate.

I searched to my front for the main target building. I couldn't identify it from the many similar compounds, so I looked for secondary features. The target was on the north end of a wide-open valley surrounded by mountains. The village sat along a meandering river. I couldn't see the water, but the sprawling, lush vegetation to my left indicated we were on course. I counted creeks. "There," I said. "Look just to the left of that dirt road parallel to our course. There is a trapezoidal-shaped compound."

"Got it," Rich said.

"Look just past it. Our LZ is the open area past that compound, just shy of the dry creek that heads up the mountain – land there."

Rich approached as gunfire erupted from a tiny goat pen to my left. A man with an AK-47 rifle ducked for cover as my left gunner returned fire. Braaaaaaap, Braaaaaap – the M-134 roared as we touched down. "Maxim Two-One is on the ground."

"Ramp clear down," I said over the intercom.

"Ramp down, unloading assaulters at this time. The last man's on the ramp – ramps up, aft ready."

"Forward Ready – Clear for flight."

I waited until I heard each chalk call down to avoid a collision before taking off. "Rich, bring her up and accelerate straight ahead at 80 knots." As he pulled in power, I keyed my mic, "Two-One – coming out – Two-One – Clear of the dust."

+++

Even with the initial shots fired, our assaulters encountered minimal resistance. We orbited nearby in case of a CASEVAC or emergency exfil, but it wasn't long before I got the call that the Objective was secure and Sensitive Site Exploitation (SSE) was ongoing.

While holding to the west, we received a call from the assault force commander stating that Scallop was not only in custody but also positively identified our other HVT, Objective Salmon. They'd been meeting without our inside sources' knowledge. With both targeted individuals captured, we could turn our attention elsewhere in the coming days.

After exfil of the assault force, two HVTs, and ten military-age males (MAMs), we returned to Bagram to hand over our detainees to the detention team and debrief our actions.

One of the mission's copilots was Otter, a former Navy SEAL and recent Green Platoon graduate. He patted me on the back as we returned from the flight line to our compound.

"Al, THAT was awesome."

"Yeah, you think?"

"Hell, yes. That was a serious adrenaline fix." He took a breath before continuing. "When we rolled in from the RP and your guns lit off, I saw your tracers rip that shed to pieces while we landed. Holy crap, that was exciting."

"They're not always that wild."

"How did you stay so calm when that dust storm engulfed us? I would have been freaking out, but you were so professional and methodical on the radio; I figured we do this all the time."

I wanted to set realistic expectations for him. "IIMC is not something I like doing with a flight; heck, I don't like doing it single-ship – but we're here, and it all worked out, so let's go do the AAR and get some chow. I'm hungry."

Not only did we succeed in getting both of our targeted individuals on a single period of darkness (POD), but my new guys validated their training for themselves and me. Green Platoon training was a crown jewel of the 160th SOAR and would remain so throughout my tenure and beyond.

Chapter 6

The Crew

Sharana, Afghanistan – Winter, 2011

The bitter cold disappeared as I added classified documents to the fire burning inside the specially designated burn barrel. Planning for missions tended to generate piles of secret trash that never made it into a mission folder. Those rejects and post-mission products needed to be destroyed. A crosscut shredder chops or grounds packets and imagery into tiny diamond-shaped bits, but if we were busy flying every night, we might not have time to shred everything before leaving the wire again. Before long, the accumulation of classified material would fill a large trash can. Shredding it would take too long, so burning it on a quiet night was the next best option, but I didn't want to do it alone, so I went inside to get some help.

I tossed a balled-up piece of imagery at my Flight Engineer's head.

Staff Sergeant Dan Devine sat about 10 feet away in our planning area. The wad of paper bounced off his headphones and onto the keyboard of his laptop computer. It looked like he was watching a movie: Yup, a romantic comedy for sure.

"Dan, want to help me burn some classified? I spoke with the customers. There's nothing on deck unless the Rangers dig up some trouble during their ground movement tonight in Salerno." I playfully tossed another piece of crumpled imagery in his direction. "I want to go outside and get some air. What do you say?"

Slowly placing his headphones on his desk, he rose with a smile. "Got a lighter or matches?"

"It's already burning. I'll meet you back at the barrel. Come on out."

Dan approached out of the darkness with two more garbage bags stuffed with sensitive documents. "Al, I think this is going to take a while."

"Yeah, but look up at the stars. What an awesome night to be out here." I tossed more material into the flames. "When you were growing up in Missouri, did you have a view of the sky like this?"

He surveyed the sky and dropped the bags near the fire. "No, the last place I saw this many stars was 2001 in the Philippines."

If nothing else, Afghanistan has a majesty and beauty that is nearly unmatched elsewhere in the world. I usually viewed the area at night through my NVGs, keeping the true allure of the mountains muted through a monochromatic yellowish-green tint. But looking up using only my eyes revealed the beauty of the night sky.

"Hey, Dan, I'm heading to the aircraft parking area tomorrow to adjust gear while the sun is up. What's a good time?"

"I'll go down with you at 13:00. The armorer's going to clean the miniguns, and I want to ensure the crew gets them set up and ready to go for the night."

"That sounds good to me. I'll use that opportunity to clean my rifle and change my laser and sight batteries."

About three hours after we started the fire, the last item turned to ash. Burn pits and burn barrels seemed like a good idea at the time, but now there are potential related health maladies tied to their use, but that's for another conversation.

+++

My alarm clock woke me to begin my next duty cycle. The sun was still up, but would go down soon enough to start our next period of darkness (POD). I didn't want to climb out of my warm sleeping bag, but I had to get moving.

I stepped out of my darkened Quonset hut into the bright daylight. I squinted as I walked toward the shower building. An inch of snow had fallen after I went to sleep. Even in the cold February air, I wore only a t-shirt, black gym shorts, and shower shoes, otherwise known as flip flops. A quick shower and shave put me in the right mindset to begin the duty day. For the most part, I enjoyed FOB life – no extraneous administrative duties got in the way of mission performance. We were chasing bad guys nearly every night, and although we didn't fly during the previous POD, I was confident we'd leave the wire this evening.

First, I wanted to grab a coffee, read my emails, and see if the SEALs were tracking potential targets for the night.

Dan walked in as I poured my second cup of coffee.

"Good morning, sir. Anything on deck?"

I cringed at the first sip of the hot black liquid. *Who made this? "It's pretty rough,"* I thought, then pointed Dan toward the large sixty-inch monitors at the front of the room. "I plotted the locations of each ISR platform, and two of the three shown are within thirty minutes' flight time. The other is way up north near Kunduz, which doesn't fit the SEAL's target set." I motioned for him to follow me to the joint operation center (JOC) next door.

"Sir, is it okay for me to be here?" he asked.

"It is if I say you belong. I like you to know what and why we're doing things. It helps with your overall situational awareness during short-notice or in-extremis missions. I can get away with explaining less to you because you'll already know the context of a target. That way, I can allocate more time to discussing actions on the objective – know what I mean?"

"Yup," was all he said as we entered the JOC.

"Notice that the same two ISR feeds we watched are displayed here. One is a vehicle follow, and the other is a compound. Mark my words; one or both will be our target tonight."

After confirming my assessment with the intel officer, Dan and I hopped into our Toyota Hilux pickup truck for a five-minute drive to the Chinook parking area. We could get there quicker in a pinch, but there was no hurry. The Toyota Tacoma-like truck bounced over the pothole-riddled dirt road with ease. I enjoyed driving it because the steering wheel was on the right vs. left with the stick shift in my left hand. Some of the younger guys had never driven a stick shift car, let alone driven it from the right seat.

Three MH-47Gs came into view as we pulled next to the trailer-like maintenance shed. The crew chiefs hung out in the plywood office structure when they weren't working on the helicopters, but for now, they were crawling all over the Chinooks like ants on a glazed doughnut.

Dan and I left our heavy coats in the truck and walked toward the MH-47 marked with a large number '51' in the second round window from the front. The number coincided with our tactical callsign, Thunder Five-One.

Walking up the ramp, I noticed how warm it was for a February day. Even at our elevation of 5,800 feet, it had to be at least 35 degrees Fahrenheit. The smell of warm hydraulic fluid filled the cabin as Sergeant Bill Jones wiped up a spill in the middle of the floor.

"Shit, Sir, watch out, this spot is slippery. I knocked over an open can of fluid, and I didn't get to it quickly enough. It's all over the place."

The young crew chief had a stack of white shop towels soaking up the viscous red fluid. I reached out to grab one. "Bill, can I have one of these? I've got to blow my nose and get rid of dust boogers."

He handed me a clean towel and returned to the mess at hand.

Dan, Bill, and I had several deployments together and were very familiar with each other. If Dan, as the Flight Engineer, was the leader of the enlisted crew, Bill was second in command. Dan's crew station was at the front right cabin door, a position known as Right Gun. He manned the M-134 on the right side, controlled the air refueling panel and the rescue hoist, and was responsible for primary hovering directional instructions to the pilots.

Bill, at the right ramp, was responsible for loading and unloading the passengers, whether or not we were conducting an assault or supply run. We had two other crew chiefs; both were E-4 gunners. Specialist Jeremy Wilson manned the left minigun, and his responsibilities included airspace surveillance and aircraft self-defense.

I looked around the aircraft for our left ramp gunner but didn't see him. "Jeremy, where's Tim?"

"Sir, he's up top servicing the aft rotor head with oil."

"Okay, thanks. Hey, do you mind if I clean my rifle over there?"

"No problem, Sir. Let me get your M-4 out of the weapon's case."

I watched as he removed my rifle from a locked box containing all seven of our long guns.

I sat on a canvas bench seat, field-stripped my M-4, and inspected and cleaned the parts while I watched Jeremy set up his M-134 at the left gun window. He deliberately weaved the ammunition belt of 7.62 MM ammunition back and forth, folding it gently as he loaded both of his ammo cans. Sometimes, we only flew with one can per side to save weight, but the terrain elevations around FOB Sharana weren't terribly high – 6,000 to 12,000 feet on average.

While observing Jeremy at work, I squirted rifle lubricant on my M-4 bolt carrier assembly and wiped it carefully.

He fed the end of the belt through the ammunition feed chute, then let it sit while he moved to the gun itself. The six-barreled Dillon M-134 minigun sits roughly waist-high on a hinged arm and is powered by a floor-mounted battery that trickle-charges between trigger pulls.

Satisfied with my rifle bolt, I moved on to the barrel and slid a lubricated cleaning rod in and out, changing patches after a few pulls. But I was still interested in watching Jeremy.

He closed and latched the safing sector housing cover, then temporarily disconnected the electric cannon plug at the ammo can's booster motor and pushed the thumb trigger, causing the empty gun to spin. "Alright, everything works," he said under his breath. Then he fed the bullets protruding from the chute into the feeder-delinker and reconnected the cannon plug.

"Jeremy, do you have to 'time' the gun?"

"No, sir, the gun has an auto-timing clutch. The old AC-powered guns needed manual timing, but these DC guns are easy-peasy." The gun was mission-ready, though we didn't have one to fly yet, so he removed the safing sector housing cover and placed it into a soundproofing pocket on the right side of the door for easy access – the gun wouldn't fire without it installed.

While he was putting the final touches on his setup, I finished assembling my rifle and added fresh batteries to my AN/PEQ-2 IR laser and Aimpoint red dot sight.

"Bill, I'm gonna set my rifle in its cockpit mount for tonight. Is that okay?"

"Sure thing, Sir. After I get the other minigun setup, I'll put everyone's rifle in place".

+++

Satisfied the helicopter was ready for action, Dan and I drove back to the planning area to await orders we knew would come around dark.

When I entered the planning area, the same ISR videos were streaming on the monitors at the front of the room. Mike, my XO, was pacing near a large whiteboard on the right side of the room.

"Mike, what's up?"

"Hey, Al, I'm trying to figure out which FOBs have functional fuel points tonight."

That was something different to ponder. "What do you mean?"

"I got an email from the S-3 that a bad batch of fuel was delivered to four fuel points in our AO."

"What do you mean, bad – contaminated?"

"Yup. It looks like we're okay here, and Ghazni looks fine. We can't go to Asadabad, Qalat, Bagram, or Shank."

"Have you checked to see if any Tankers are available for air refueling if needed?"

"I did, and there are two tankers available from Bagram. They have fuel from a previous shipment. We can have them if needed, but I was asked not to utilize them unless there were no other options."

Well, it was nice to have them available if needed, but based on the targets that I knew the SEALs were evaluating, we had plenty of gas for the night.

Sergeant Steve Sarloc, our intelligence NCO, appeared from his secure room behind the monitors. "Mister Mack, can you come back to the SCIF? I want to show you something."

Deployment humor is usually crude but seems funny at the time. "I'll come back there, but you've got to keep your clothes on." Then I added, "This time."

He smiled before replying. "I'll behave if I can have a backrub."

"You got it," I said as I headed his way.

Once in the SCIF, he closed the door and turned up the volume on his music player to provide background noise. "The vehicle-follow on monitor number two is tonight's target. We're still waiting for the occupants to head toward their usual bed-down location before the assault force wants to launch." He pointed to a map on his desk. "Through the ISR feed, we observed them planting improvised explosive devices in the road leading here to Sharana."

Just then, the SEAL Master Chief walked in. "Al, we want you to interdict the car we've been monitoring. They laid explosives outside our FOB, and we've intercepted a push-to-talk (PTT) communication that says they're planning on ambushing an American patrol."

"Where is the ambush? Do we know?"

"They're racing to get into position ahead of a small convoy of fuel trucks headed to replace the supply at Shank."

I glanced at my wristwatch. "Let me talk to my boss, and we'll meet at the helicopters ASAP. You can have a load of twenty-five assaulters per Chinook." He didn't complain; that was our typical ACL for this time of year.

As I walked out of the SCIF, I alerted the guys that we had a mission, and Mike immediately started marking up the dry-erase board and assigning duties to the other pilots. "Dan," he said. "Can you call the flight line and get the crew chiefs out to the aircraft, get the APUs on, then run the checklists up to engine start?"

"Yes, Sir."

While my team prepared for a Time-Sensitive Target (TST), I had to brief Captain Mark Barton, my officer-in-charge (OIC), on the plan. Once I laid things out, he called our headquarters at Bagram to get permission to launch, which he received.

I gathered the pilots and flight engineers near the monitors at the front of the room. "Okay, guys, this vehicle is our target." I pointed at the ISR feed, then tapped a map on the wall, indicating where it was and the direction of travel. "He's heading easterly, so we'll take off to the southwest, test fire guns, loop back to the right, and start a tail-chase. The ISR platform we're looking at is a pair of A-10s, Hawg Two-One and Hawg Two-Two. Not only will they 'talk us on' and laze the vehicle, but they'll provide fire support." I shuffled through a stack of papers. "The observed weather: The moon has already set, so we're looking at zero illum. The temperature is 2 degrees Celsius, the pressure altitude is 6,000 feet, and the wind is from the northeast at 10 knots. The forecast shows no changes for the next forty-eight hours."

I glanced over my shoulder at the monitor one last time. "I'll lead as Thunder Five-One, Sassy; You'll fly as Thunder Five-Two. I want you in a free cruise formation when we take off – three to five disks. At one mile from the target vehicle, I want you to tighten up and assume staggered right."

Sassy nodded as I continued. "If the vehicle is underway, my right gunner will perform the stop, then I'll loop around to the left and clear the target so you can infil your assaulters at the vehicle's seven to five o'clock. Make sure your left gun has a clear field of fire when you touch down. I'll return to target and land at your eight o'clock, perpendicular to your heading in an 'L' with my right gun on target. Then we'll play things by ear." I sipped my coffee. *Yuck, cold*, I thought. "If the vehicle stops before we interdict, I'll land where I need to and call my heading. You land simultaneously at my four o'clock in an 'L.' Ensure gunners identify their targets and make sure fires and the effects of fires have a clear line. Joe, you'll be bringing up the rear in Thunder Five-Three. You hold about a half mile to the west, left turns, and wait for instructions."

I looked around the room. Everyone's game face was appropriate and in place. "Okay, other than what I just briefed, everything is per our standard Sharana brief and the TAC SOP. If there are no questions, let's roll."

+++

Before slipping out the door, I donned a long-sleeve thermal undershirt under my uniform top. Then, we all piled into our individual Hilux trucks and hauled ass to the aircraft. I wanted to ensure we beat the SEALS; otherwise, they'd already be loaded, and I'd have to climb up and squeeze into the aircraft through the cabin door and under the minigun instead of walking up the ramp.

We parked the trucks as we did earlier in the day and jogged to our aircraft. The enlisted crew had the auxiliary power units running, navigation systems were online, and all the fancy computers, black boxes, and hydraulics were tested and ready to go. All I had to do was strap into my seat and start the engines. Conventional Army units would never allow crew chiefs to perform these duties, but our guys were well-trained, making remarkably short timelines for takeoff possible.

I looked down the line of parked Chinooks. Each aircraft had identifying chemsticks laid out on the ground at the ramp. One for Chalk One, Two for Chalk Two, and you guessed it, Three for Chalk Three. This simple marking made it easy for the SEALS to identify which aircraft they were to load, because sometimes, the helicopters could be out of order based on how they'd been towed from the clamshell hangar.

I, like everyone else, took the opportunity to urinate in the bushes, possibly the last chance to go for several hours. Then I walked up the ramp, slipped on my ballistically protected flight vest, swapped holsters for my pistol, and entered the blue-lit cockpit. The loud whine of the APU turbine hurt my ears until I donned my flight helmet and buckled my safety harness. My helmet was already plugged in, and the radios were busy with chatter involving our vehicle interdiction.

My crew was all business as the assault force began loading. "Sir, the ground force commander is about to plug into the ICS."

"Thanks for the heads up, Dan."

"Al, It's Lou. I'm plugged in and brought twenty-four Eagles with me. How do we look?"

I keyed my floor mic, updated him on the target vehicle's location and speed, and confirmed the other Chinooks were loaded and we already had 'launch authority.'

Tim let me know he was ready to fire up the engines. "Posted on Number One, and rotors are clear."

"Roger," I said as I flipped the left-side fuel pumps on and opened the crossfeed valve. "Fuel Pressure Lights are out". I moved the left-side engine condition lever to the ground detent. "One to motor," I announced.

Tim acknowledged. "Roger, One to start."

I tipped the engine start switch to the left and held it until the gas turbine indicator showed 10%. "NG is 10% and climbing." The turbine engine was now in an automated start sequence. "NG is stable at 50%, and engine oil pressure is above 5 PSI – good start on One."

Bill was ready on the right-hand side. "Sir, posted on Number Two."

I repeated the process, and once I was satisfied the engines were running normally, I advanced the overhead engine condition levers slowly to the flight detent. The smooth application of power spun the dual rotors up to their operating RPM. With a few more pre-flight checks complete, we were ready to go, but now I had to wait for the other crews to check in, which didn't take long.

"Thunder Five-One, this is Thunder Five-Three – Up with twenty-five Eagles and one dog."

"Five-One copies."

"Thunder Five-One, this is Thunder Five-Two – Up with twenty-five Eagles and one dog."

"Five-One copies. Break – Thunder Flight, push button three on Victor for ATC, pitch-pull will occur five seconds after clearance."

"Sharana Tower, Thunder Flight located at Cougar Ramp, flight of three Forty-Sevens, request takeoff to the west with immediate frequency change."

"Thunder Flight, Sharana Tower, Wind is Zero Six Zero at ten, from present position – cleared for takeoff with immediate frequency change approved."

"Mike, if you don't mind, I'd like to fly."

"No problem. You have the controls."

I flexed my gloved hands and lightly grabbed the flight controls. I tapped the brake release with both toes, increased power with my left hand, and simultaneously eased the cyclic stick forward with my right. The result was a climbing, accelerating Chinook in the dark with two others in tow.

Captain Barton called the lead A-10 to let him know we were in the air and en route. "Hawg Two-One, this is Thunder Eight-One; we're a flight of three MH-47s. We departed from FOB Sharana and are proceeding to intercept the vehicle you're following – request a SITREP."

I could hear the A-10 pilot reply, but just barely, so, by touch, I found the UHF radio knob and turned up the volume ever so slightly.

"Thunder, Hawg Two-One SITREP: One SUV with several armed occupants is proceeding northbound at approximately thirty miles per hour. The current grid is 42S VB 89451 81910. In about a mile, their road will intercept a larger one; from there, they could go southwest or northeast."

"Hawg Two-One, Thunder copies all – Out."

"Alright, Sir, good job. Guys, Weapons control status is Free." I looked around the cockpit before speaking again. "Mike, let's turn off our external lights, dim the cockpit lighting, and ensure the missile warning system is set to auto-dispense."

We couldn't have been more ready. But as we closed the distance, the vehicle stopped.

"Thunder, Hawg Two-One on Fires. The vehicle stopped at 42S VB 90073 83446 near a grove of trees, and five armed men got out and headed for the vegetation. The SUV is stationary with what appears to be an armed Military Aged Male (MAM) on the passenger side. Use caution as you approach."

"Hawg Two-One, Thunder Flight is one minute out – Sparkle on."

The lead A-10 pilot pointed an IR laser at the vehicle to help confirm we were heading for the correct vehicle. "Sparkle on," he replied, and a thin laser beam, only visible through NVGs, came down from the heavens onto the roof of the targeted SUV.

"Sparkle off," I said once I was satisfied with the ID.

I set the aircraft brakes so we wouldn't roll on touchdown and keyed the radio from my cyclic stick trigger. "Thunder Flight, this is Five-One. The vehicle is stationary; we'll land in an 'L.' My heading is three-three-zero – beginning approach now."

Dan opened fire as I began my descent and deceleration.

Brrrrrraaaap! Brrrrraaaaap! "Right Gun engaging. We're taking fire from the car and the wood line."

Bill joined in on the Right Rear M-240. Instead of 3,000 rounds a minute, his machine gun's cyclic rate of fire was closer to 700 rounds a minute.

As I approached 80 feet above the ground, I knew I wouldn't get much help from the crew with coordination.

Tim picked up the calls, and Dan and Bill were busy with the guns. "We're off 60 feet, heavy dust forming at the ramp."

I ensured the hover page was selected on my inboard MFD and kept the velocity vector straight and my VSI at 300 feet per minute.

Brrrrrraaaap! Brrrrrraaaap!

"Dust mid-cabin, you're off twenty."

Ideally, I wanted my speed to match half my altitude. "We're doing 8 knots, showing 16 feet on the RADALT."

I glanced out the window one last time before committing entirely to the instruments and saw several tracers fly past the nose of the helicopter. The minigun didn't scare them; they were still trying to shoot us down. We'd have to kill them to make them stop, and Dan was giving it his best as he raked the stationary car. The aft gear touched the ground, and I lowered the helicopter's nose until the forward landing gear touched down. "Thunder Five-One is on the ground," I announced on the internal frequency. "Ramp Clear Down," I said.

Bill was already on it. "Ground Contact lights illuminated – Ramp Down – Eagles unloading at this time." I sat nervously, waiting for the assault force to disembark so I could get back into the air. We were highly vulnerable, sitting there in the dark with suspended dust in the air.

Another minigun blast ripped the target vehicle, and both of the left side doors flew into the air as the bullets chewed through the metal. The enemy combatant near the car was dead, and Dan shifted his attention to the tree line that Thunder Five-Two's guns were engaging. The gunners wanted to stay put, but the SEALS couldn't move on to the objective until we stopped firing, so I pulled pitch and joined Thunder Five-Three a mile away in holding.

The SEALs moved to contact with the enemy in the grove of trees. Two of the enemy were dead, but the other three were protected from machine gun and rifle fire by a small stone structure. That wouldn't hold up for long with HAWG overhead. The JTAC coordinated a bomb run followed by a strafe with the thirty-millimeter cannon. It wasn't long before the call on the radio was objective secure, SSE in progress.

Twenty minutes later, we were still holding nearby when the exfil call came over the radio. The SEALS left the five E-KIAs where they fell, brought back a laptop, maps, and documents, and destroyed a cache of ammunition and explosive bomb-making materials.

+++

Retrieving the assault force was uneventful, as was the return to FOB Sharana. The fuelers were waiting to top off the helicopters to their pre-determined quantity. The crew chiefs verified there were no bullet holes or other damage to the helicopters, and we pilots finished the adrenaline-filled night with the mundane task of logging the flight hours in the maintenance laptop computers.

"I'm hungry," I said to the others. "Let's hit the mess hall, get breakfast, and return to pre-flight the helicopters." It seems as if the highlights of my deployments were food and sleep. Make both of those quality events, and I could go on forever.

Breakfast was probably the best meal of the day – eggs to order, bacon, fresh fruit, juice, and hot coffee made for a tasty meal. While we ate, the crew chiefs conducted their detailed PMD inspection before our less intense pre-flight inspection. I would describe the PMD as a functional-mechanical inspection, whereas the pre-flight was more of a second set of eyes before buttoning up the covers, cowlings, and doors.

After breakfast, before I stood 20 feet in the air atop the aft pylon work platform and marveled at Afghanistan's beauty. The sun peaked over the mountain range to our east, with a slight pink hue in the sky and a glint of sunlight hitting the snow-covered mountains to the west. A slight breeze tickled the back of my neck, and there was no smoke from the refuse burn pit for once.

"Al, are you done up there?" Mike wanted to get back to the planning area to complete our debrief so he could get some sleep.

"Yeah, I'll be right down." I surveyed the landscape one more time as the sun climbed higher. *Time for bed*, I thought. After all, we are Night Stalkers and fly Chinooks in the dark. Daylight brings out the 'daywalkers' and their frivolous rules. "Let's go," I said as I climbed down the side of my helicopter.

My sleeping bag is calling.

Chapter 7

FMQ

Kabul, Afghanistan – October 2008

I talked earlier about Basic Mission Qualified Pilots (BMQ) and their role as junior pilots, regardless of rank. They can act as copilots in any Chalk other than the lead aircraft. Their pilot-in-command (PIC) has an FMQ rating, meaning they are Fully Mission Qualified, can participate in any customer support missions, and can perform all tasks and maneuvers used by the 160th SOAR.

If not acting as a PIC, an FMQ may perform duties as a Flight Lead's copilot, which is where this story comes from. CW3 Cal Dockery, the man I assessed earlier in this book, recounted a hostage rescue mission from Afghanistan. The hostage, Mister Smith, not his real name, from the US Army Corps of Engineers, was kidnapped along with his interpreter. Smith, an engineer working on a dam project, was abducted in mid-August by a militant Islamic group not affiliated with Al Qaeda or the Taliban. Criminal gunmen killed Smith's driver and threatened to do the same to him if his wife didn't pay a substantial ransom.

Negotiations continued into the Fall as his wife tried to raise money, intending to pay the ransom as soon as she accumulated the correct sum, even though the FBI recommended not paying. Meanwhile, US intelligence assets cast a wide net to find and retrieve Mister Smith.

In late September, his whereabouts narrowed to a potential location, and the Special Operations Task Force in Jalalabad was assigned to rescue him.

Cal described the planning that went into the operation as deliberate, detailed, and frustrating. You see, the hostage location kept changing. They were all in the same general area, but a 400–500 meter difference in Afghanistan might mean an elevation of 5,000 feet vs. 9,000 feet. That can be a difference in combat load (ACL) of thirty assaulters or ten. It also can mean climbing a mountain or running from a helicopter to a compound's front door – two very different tactics and timing. Only time and an accurate source would tell.

The first and second planning days produced five options with very different tactics. Brandon, the Flight Lead, sat with the pilots to discuss how he wanted to proceed. "Look," he said. "Two targets require landing to the 'X,' and three are offset infils." He tapped his finger on the map. "The 'X' targets are simple. They're relatively rural, so we only need to land in the open spaces between buildings, and the elevations are roughly equal, so the ACLs are the same. Flight time is the only difference by about twenty minutes." He looked at the faces staring back and passed out assignments. "Cal, you plan the ridgeline target southwest of Kabul; Craig, you take the target near Ghazni; and Bill, plan for the mountain near Gardez."

The FMQs separated and got to work refining routes and fuel numbers for their assigned objectives.

+++

The FBI relayed a crucial message regarding Mister Smith: His wife must pay his ransom within twenty-four hours, or she could have his lifeless body back.

The national intelligence apparatus kicked into high gear, confirming his whereabouts with a high degree of certainty – the high ridgeline to the southwest of Kabul. Brandon got Cal's attention. "Let's call this Objective Ridge Runner."

"You've got it, boss," said Cal as he shuffled anything unrelated away from the main planning table and pigeonholed it in a safe place in case the materials were required later. Then, he and the others frantically pieced together what they'd need for the night. Meanwhile, the Flight Lead and SEAL commander discussed the danger of compromise due to the robust enemy early warning network in and around Kabul. The Chinooks would conduct a nighttime offset infil of the assault force just after nightfall. The HLZ on the valley floor would allow an easy landing, but the enemy defenders would likely detect the helicopters and kill Mister Smith long before the SEALs could scale the formidable terrain.

"Deception." Brandon paused as he confirmed the idea in his mind. "Deception is the only way," he said matter-of-factly. He moved to one of the whiteboards, erased non-relevant information, and scribbled out his plan with a green dry-erase marker before conducting his hasty AMB.

While the crews finalized their maps and imagery markings, overhead assets arrived in a stack several thousand feet above the enemy encampment. Cal and the other pilots headed to their respective aircraft while Brandon called the Task Force Commander for a final back-brief. Mister Smith would either be dead or free during this period of darkness (POD).

+++

As the Flight Lead's copilot, Cal ensured the Chinook and crew were ready to go when Brandon and the SEALs arrived. So, he walked around the aircraft, flashlight in hand, to confirm all access panels and doors were closed and latched. All the 'Remove Before Flight' pins and flags were stowed correctly, and mission equipment and armament were configured and ready to go: M-134 miniguns – Check, External hoist – Check, Cabin seats removed – Check.

Satisfied that the hardware was ready, he donned his body armor and flight helmet and slid into the right cockpit seat, quickly fastening his harness. The auxiliary power unit was already running with the APU generator engaged. He now analyzed each equipment status page in the flight management software; Global Positioning Systems and Inertial Navigation Systems were aligned and ready for flight. He checked in with the other two Chinooks and conducted the COMMEX. Nothing was left to do but obsessively go over everything again until his Flight Lead arrived.

Moments after Brandon strapped into his seat, the SATCOM crackled to life. "Bronson Four-One, this is Bronson Base; you have 'Launch Authority' for Objective Ridge Runner. Acknowledge."

"Bronson Base, Bronson Four-One, confirms receipt of 'Launch Authority.' Break – Bronson flight, Check in with Eagle Count and status."

"Four-One, this is Four-Three. I have four Eagles and am ready for engine start." His four passengers were doctors making up a surgical resuscitation team.

"Four-One, this is Four-Two. I have twenty Eagles and one dog – ready for engine start." His passengers made up a Quick Reaction Force (QRF).

"Flight this is Four-One. I have twenty-five Eagles and one dog." This ground force was composed entirely of Navy SEALs and one K-9. "Push button three on 'Victor' for ATC, button nineteen on 'Uniform' for fires, and maintain internal on 'Fox Mike.' Start engines and let me know when you are ready to depart."

The Air Traffic Controller had difficulty seeing the black Chinooks in the dark, so he donned a pair of Night Vision Goggles and cleared them for takeoff when they called.

Cal took off from JBAD and headed west. His seatbelt strained against the turbulence. *"Wow, this sucks,"* he thought. The wind was stronger out of the west than forecast. "Brandon, the wind is whipping around 40 knots. I'll hold about 150 to maintain our time."

"Do whatever you need to do, Cal."

The downside to the strong wind was a bumpy flight, but there was a healthy upside. The sound of the helicopters would be considerably masked by the howling wind, which should help the deception plan now unfolding. After test-firing the guns, the second and third Chinooks started backing away from the lead helicopter and then each other. With thirty seconds of separation between each aircraft, there was time for Lead to descend out of formation, land, unload the assault force, and climb back up into the trail position while the other two continued as if flying a routine resupply mission – a brilliant concept executed with precision. Overhead intelligence assets confirmed that the deceptive infil was not detected or reported by enemy early warning or sentries.

Bronson Four-Two led the flight of three, minus the primary assault team of SEALs, back to their pre-planned laager site at nearby FOB Airborne. Once there, they'd refuel, shut down to Readiness Level Two, and eat while the SEALs climbed nearly 3,000 feet to the targeted area. The orbiting overhead stack grew as the ISR platforms were joined by an AC-130 gunship, a pair of A-10s, F-15Es, and another armed unmanned aerial vehicle (UAV).

Level Two required the crew to remain in the Chinook with the APU on, systems aligned, ready to restart, and depart within two to three minutes – a prime opportunity to eat and stretch.

Cal stepped out into the chilly night air and shivered as the howling wind made urinating challenging. It would be a long, miserable night if he peed on his uniform. While completing nature's call, he noticed a Toyota Hilux pull up to each Chinook, delivering food trays to the hungry aviators. He wondered aloud about what they'd be eating. Their last meal had been two pieces of stale white bread, a slice of bologna, and yellow American cheese with no condiments or seasoning. *"No, thank you,"* he thought.

"Sir," his Flight Engineer said, "They sent us buffalo chicken wings."

"Cool," he said.

Unfortunately for Cal's stomach, the SEALs made better time than anyone predicted.

Brandon shouted for Cal to get back in his seat. "The ground force is at the LCC (Last Cover and Concealment), and it sounds like they're moving without delay."

Cal turned up the volume of the UHF radio just in time to hear, "Assault in progress."

Like a scene from an action movie, the ground force quietly began killing the sentries with silenced weapons as they entered the security perimeter. The radio operator whispered, "Shots fired." A short moment later, he whispered again, Two EKIA – make that three."

Several more EKIAs went down before the assault force called "Objective Secure, SSE in progress." Sensitive Site Exploitation would reveal the fate of Mister Smith. Then Cal heard the codeword they'd been waiting to hear – "Jackpot, I say again, Jackpot."

"Precious Cargo is secure and well. Launch the exfil helo for the primary exfil HLZ."

Brandon instructed the other two Chinooks to remain at nearby FOB Airborne, simplifying the air plan over the objective. He intended to hoist Mister Smith into the aircraft because there was nowhere to land on top of the craggy ridgeline.

So far, everything was going to plan with flawless execution, and it probably would have continued that way. Still, a famous quote from a nineteenth century Prussian field marshal states, "No plan survives contact with the enemy," and things were about to become more difficult.

"Bronson Four-One, this is Uniform-One. The P.C. wants to walk out. He doesn't want to ride the hoist. How copy?"

Cal knew that was a bad idea. Mister Smith's prison was the most level ground on the mountain. Everywhere else, serrated outcroppings and sharp ditches made up the rugged, steep-sloping terrain. Once they started down, he figured the poorly nourished man would collapse within a few hundred meters, and he was correct. The SEALs hadn't walked more than twenty minutes when Mister Smith slowed, stopped, and sat on a small boulder. He was breathless and could go no further – neither down nor up.

"Bronson Four-One, Uniform-One, HLZ 'Black' at our current location. We're going to need a hoist exfil."

Cal turned his helicopter and approached the waiting men, intentionally heading into the wind. "*Damn*", he thought," *This is gonna suck.*" He came to an appropriate hover height for hoisting, but as he slowed to a stop, he looked around frantically for a visual reference that would allow him to maintain his position. The wind gusts varied from zero wind to 50 knots, making stationary hovering challenging. Cal doubted he could hold the aircraft stationary and stable enough to hoist.

If Cal's skills weren't already tested, they were when the wind shifted.

Blowing dust roiled into his field of view, forcing him to pivot in a new direction. "*Why hadn't they just stayed with the original plan?*" he thought. "*Things would have been so much simpler.*" Cal strained to look down the cable to the Jungle Penetrator over his right shoulder. Mister Smith sat on the folding seat, hugging the vertical support, gripped by fear.

As the hoisted hostage reached the door, a massive downdraft dropped the massive Chinook 3 or 4 feet. Cal felt the right aft landing gear bump into a nearby stone pillar. Bump isn't the correct word; smash is more appropriate. Caution lights illuminated in the cockpit, and 'Bitching Betty' let them know a problem existed. "*Check Cautions, Check Cautions.*"

The utility hydraulic segment in the Warnings, Caution, and Advisory page was telltale. His landing gear was damaged enough to leak hydraulic fluid. "*Damn,*" he thought. "*This adds a wrinkle that we don't need.*"

Oblivious to the problem, Mister Smith climbed into the helicopter with a big smile. He was free, alive, and going home to his wife.

The flight still had some challenges getting the assault force off the mountain, with some additional minor damage occurring to the Chinook's underside, but in the end, no rescuers were injured, and the P.C. was safe, happy, and going home.

That ending is as good as any Night Stalker can ask for.

Chapter 8

Air Mission Commander

Sharana, June 2009

Although Warrant Officers make up the majority of line pilots for the 160th, the mission assignments, selection, guidance, and administrative functions are the responsibility of the Captains, Majors, and Colonels.

Warrant officers can stay in the unit as long as they want and remain productive, but the regular commissioned officers have between three and five years unless they are selected for Command, gaining more time in the organization. I count many of these officers as respected leaders and good friends. If Warrant Officers make up the entire Flight Lead population, what remains for responsibility in flight? The Air Mission Commander has a crucial role that the regular officers typically hold.

Description of responsibilities as described in the 160th RTSOP:

Air Mission Commander (AMC): When two or more aircraft are operating as one flight, an air mission commander is responsible for the overall accomplishment of the air mission and ensuring mission accomplishment IAW the commander's intent. The AMC is responsible for unity of effort for the aviation task force and must be prepared to execute complex contingencies and fire support. He assists the Flight Lead with COA development to include contingencies.

As you can imagine, this duty can be crucial to the success of complex missions. The AMC usually sits in the Troop Commander (Jump) seat in between and slightly behind the pilots when performing duties in an MH-47 Chinook. The downside is that he has no physical control of the helicopter while potentially watching the pilots struggle with a life-or-death predicament. I've been there. That seat can be scary.

The upside is that he has the best situational awareness of the entire battle – air and ground. He can alleviate pressure on the Flight Lead by assisting in radio communications, including being a third set of ears for radio calls, backup navigation, and battle tracking. When working with a skilled and experienced AMC, I liked to divide cockpit duties, such as who handled specific radio conversations. Typically, on my flights, he'd handle the over-the-horizon communications on the SATCOM, and I'd handle all of the Line-of-Sight conversations unless I got busy, and then I'd hand off those calls to him.

Training a new Air Mission Commander in the 160th the right way can be harsh and painful. The AMC needs a personality that exudes professionalism and confidence to survive in a Warrant Officer-centric environment. He knows he's in charge and doesn't have to remind anyone because he commands the respect of his pilots, especially the Flight Lead. He must have a thick skin and take plain-spoken (blunt) critique, even when it borders on insubordination. The organization is founded and based upon candid opinions and after-action reviews (AAR). Sometimes, those comments can sting. I've been on both ends of instructional, honest, and occasionally severe corrections – sometimes earned and sometimes not. A regular officer, such as a Lieutenant or Captain, might not be used to that environment; not all can handle a warrant officer ass-chewing, but those who can thrive and rise to roles with more responsibility and eventually command.

I don't know how often I've heard a young Captain complain about a difficult situation I placed him in during training. "Al, there's no way I'll have to deal with the complexities you've presented me. I can handle any situation likely to confront us, but you're throwing too many contingencies at me. This is…"

"Sir, sorry to interrupt your pity party, but I'm showing you how a well-running mission can go off the rails in the blink of an eye. I need you to learn how to roll with the punches and pay attention to all aspects of the mission, including the ground force locations, timing of their actions on the objective, status of fuel and ammunition of all the enablers and fire platforms."

He'd be mad but remain tight-lipped. After all, I was the Flight Lead during multiple combat tours. There must be some value in learning from me.

+++

Captain Mark Barton walked into the FOB Sharana planning area and sat in his seat beside me. The sun was setting, and I was deep into the beginning of my nightly ritual – coffee, emails, Situation Reports, intelligence summaries, and analyzing the currently displayed ISR feeds. For some reason, all the surveillance and intelligence-gathering platforms were within ten miles of our location. I logged into my computer and plotted the coordinates on Falcon View flight planning software. Both locations sat a mere five miles away to the northwest and another to the northeast, roughly five to six miles apart. An equilateral triangle was formed if I connected a straight line between the targets and our location.

"Heck, Sir, the SEALs could walk to both locations as if we did an offset infil. I wonder which place they'll hit tonight. Let's go next door to the TOC and gauge atmospherics."

"Won't they just come over and get you when they're ready?"

"Yes, Sir, they will, but if we're involved in the operation's initial planning process and overall concept, we can eliminate any stupid requests before they form. It's easier to convince the ground force not to do something before they fall in love with it."

"Got it. I'm in."

I'm glad we went because the guys were cooking up some exciting plans, none of which would be good for the helicopters. The SEALs intended to hit both Objectives during this single period of darkness, but wanted to strike them sequentially. First, they'd do an offset infil to the northeast target; let's call that Objective One. Once done, we'd exfil them and hop the three-minute flight to the 'X' on the northwest target; let's call that Objective Two – the names for the purpose of this story aren't fancy or creative but simple and effective. I can't say I liked the plan. Despite the proximity, there wasn't enough time to conduct both hits before sunrise. So, I proposed a less time-consuming and much sportier option.

"Gentlemen, I've got an idea you might like."

The Commander, the Troop Chief, and the key planners looked up from the table full of target imagery, slightly irritated at my interruption.

"Let's hit both Objectives simultaneously. We'll use two Chinooks per location, which will be plenty of lift for you. Hitting them together will eliminate any chance of tip-off to each other. You did say they're working together, right?"

The intel officer nodded in the affirmative.

"Okay, this is how we'll 'skin this cat.' I will lead a flight of two in a counterclockwise circular route, ultimately bringing us on an approach heading of two seven zero degrees. We'll be using callsigns Thunder Five-One and Thunder Five-Two. My Fourth Battalion Crew will lead the remaining flight of two, callsigns Thunder Five-Three and Thunder Five-Four, in a clockwise route. We'll land at both locations to the 'X' virtually simultaneously.

"Because the bad guys are so close to the airfield, helicopters fly over and around them all day and night, and I'm sure the smug little bastards think they're slick by setting up operations within our traffic pattern."

The SEALs expressed some concerns with airspace deconfliction but liked the idea.

"It's simple. I'll fly an arc with a seven-mile radius. After infil, I'll continue straight to the west until I pass Objective Two, giving it a wide berth before intercepting another seven-mile counterclockwise arc and returning to Sharana. There's a slight rise, a hilltop, looking out over the valley at the north end of the runway. We can see both objectives and the overhead stack from that spot." I paused to let that sink in. "We can respond to potential CASEVAC quite fast. I think you'll like how we execute this plan."

The Troop Commander nodded with a smile as I continued laying out the sequence.

"'Sassy' will lead his flight in a reciprocal pattern, but he'll keep his routing inside ours to avoid a potential head-on collision. If we have to break away for any reason, we'll turn north, and they will bank to the south." I could see smiles and nods. The SEALs were into my concept.

"I spoke with the Fires Officer. He's comfortable with two stacks, one over each Objective on separate frequencies. Look, this will be impressive; we've got two AC-130s, four A-10s, two UAVs, and one U-21 callsign Darko Two-Zero."

The SEALs accepted my plan with minor modifications, and Captain Barton and I returned to our planning area to implement it.

+++

Not long after sundown, my flight of two MH-47Gs departed FOB Sharana to the south with a second flight of two in a distant trail formation. We test-fired our guns, and each pair went its own way. My flight to the east, then northerly, and the other two turned west and toward the north.

Not every mission requires precision timing, but this one called for it. I counted my blessings that I had Captain Barton in my jump seat to share the workload. While I handled the navigation and airspace deconfliction, he spoke with Darko Two-Zero using his callsign, Thunder Eight-Zero.

I set my target imagery on my knee and listened to the AMC do his business. Not only did he get a current SITREP for our Objective, but he got one for Objective Two as well. Then he switched to fires to get a fuel endurance and weapons load-out for both stacks. We expected a gunfight in both locations based on who the targeted individuals were, so he wanted to know for sure what he had to work with. While he was coordinating the Laser and sensor tasking, a flight of two F-15Es joined us.

A check-in is relatively standard and sounded something like this: "Thunder Eight-Zero, Dude One-Five, and One-Six checking in – Two by F15Es, 18 to the south, 15,000 feet. One-Five is carrying two by high drag MK-82s – airburst, two GBU 38s – instantaneous and delayed, two by GBU 54s, and 350 rounds of twenty mike-mike. One hour and thirty minutes of playtime – FLIR, FAC-A, have products."

I liked what I heard, but he should have checked in with the stack controller, not us. I told Barton to pass Dude on to Darko, who controlled both overhead stacks as 'Warden.'

"Six minutes," I announced on the ICS. The crew and 'customers' acknowledged.

At three minutes, I could see the series of buildings, and at one minute, I was pretty sure I could see building number ten – we'd be landing with it just outside my left door. "Sir, have Darko 'laze' building ten."

Barton was on it. "Darko Two-Zero, Objective One – building Ten, Sparkle – on."

An IR laser emitting from far above pointed to the center of the primary target building.

Barton confirmed he had a visual on the building and had Darko cease the laser activity.

Joe Verner, my copilot, adjusted his speed and angle of approach before being engulfed in a thick, nasty dust cloud.

Crew coordination went as it should, and he touched down on time and in the perfect spot. The SEALs were motivated and unloaded quickly, allowing us to depart unscathed – we caught the enemy off guard on both targets, just as I'd hoped.

With both infils completed, our four Chinooks rejoined on the ground at FOB Sharana, facing the North with a great view. I didn't usually get to watch actions on the Objective, but tonight, I had a front-row seat.

+++

The ground forces had been in a firefight on Objective One since infil. So far, they'd been handling it with small arms and air-dropped munitions, but now they had to deal with a barricaded group armed with a belt-fed machine gun.

Barton hastily scribbled notes, trying to track which buildings had been cleared, where 'squirters' had run to, and which air platforms were engaging targets, and the radio traffic was heavy. So, we divided radios and nets to maintain situational awareness regarding both objectives. I focused on Objective One to the northeast, so I pulled my radio pin for Objective Two, leaving Barton to pay attention to their actions.

My assault force was moving quickly, and I tracked their progress, annotating building clearance and fire missions using a fine-tipped permanent marker on my Grid Reference Graphic, known by the acronym G.R.G. The one-meter resolution satellite imagery is broken down into two images. The Macro is an overview of the objective in which the building clusters are grouped numerically, i.e., ten series, twenty series, thirty series, etc. Ten is usually the primary target.

The most used image is the micro GRG, which breaks down the groupings by individual compounds and buildings, such as ten, eleven, twelve, thirteen, twenty-three, twenty-four, and so on. Also, each image is alphanumerically indexed starting at the top left with equidistant reference squares, designated as A, B, C, etc. Then, from top to bottom, the grid is labeled 1, 2, 3, etc.

I heard Darko call the SEALs about my objective: "Uniform-Two, this is Darko. I'm not sure if you noticed, but when the helos touched down, there were five squirters from building ten."

"Negative, Darko, we did not observe. Send locations and composition when able."

"Uniform-Two, what appears to be two armed military-aged males fled building ten and moved to building fifteen, two went to building fourteen, and one is lying prone in a small ditch south of building twenty at location Lima-Ten. How copy?"

The Air Force Combat Controller read the information back to ensure accuracy. The description was easy to follow and understand, so I marked my GRG accordingly. Barton didn't hear the call but looked over my shoulder, keeping his own tally.

The complexity of the mission increased slightly when an AC-130 fire mission started dropping artillery rounds on Objective Two. Barton's stress level was fine until my Objective added a similar attack. From our perch on the Sharana hilltop, I could see both AC-130s raining fire from above onto their respective areas. Eventually, the enemy capitulated, and Sensitive Site Exploitation began. I started nervously tapping my heel while waiting for the rollup, which came as a slant report. Objective One had ten military-aged males, twenty women, six elderly adults, fifteen children, and eight enemy killed-in-action. Over the radio, it sounds like this: "Objective One, slant as follows: ten – slant twenty – slant six – slant fifteen – slant eight. All ten MAMs will be coming off the objective; nine will exfil on Thunder Five-Two. Thunder Five-One will have a follow-on target with thirty-five Eagles."

"Another target," I announced on the ICS.

Barton had been listening while he copied the SITREPS from both Objectives. He passed word to Thunder Five-Three that his assault force was ready for exfil, and ours would hit a hasty follow-on target, which had yet to be announced.

Uniform-One passed 42S VB 94708 78004 and asked me to identify an HLZ no closer than 300 meters to the targeted compound.

I reached past my right knee and tapped my CDU keyboard to enter the target coordinates, then slewed the Multifunction Display using the digital map to look ahead. From what I could see, the follow-on Objective was another 5 miles further north with no natural hazards or culturally significant impediments. Then, I selected not a map feature, but one-meter imagery. In the center of my MFD was a walled compound, with a large orchard to the northwest and a narrow creek running east to west just to the south. I found several open areas, but one last check was the terrain contours. I selected contour lines from a button on the bezel of the MFD and rotated the contour interval selector on the CDU. Wow, the spot I selected had a steep slope, and it would be challenging to land with a heavy load of assaulters. I squeezed a button on the handle of my multi-function controller, slewed a crosshair cursor over the image, and selected a more

Two MH-47Gs fly in formation across the New Mexico desert. Note the Air Refueling Probe protruding from the right side of the helicopter's nose. Both aircraft are armed with M-134 miniguns, as seen toward the front of the cabin. (Photo provided by Boeing Helicopters)

Above: Five pilot-configurable multi-function displays (MFDs) provide information that can be displayed efficiently, improving the pilot's situational awareness. MFDs can display a split or full-screen image showing a digital and scalable moving map, RADAR, or FLIR/EOS video. (Photo provided by Alan Mack,160th SOAR)

Below: An MH-47E lands at night using Night Vision Goggles (NVG). (Photo provided by Alan Mack, 160th SOAR)

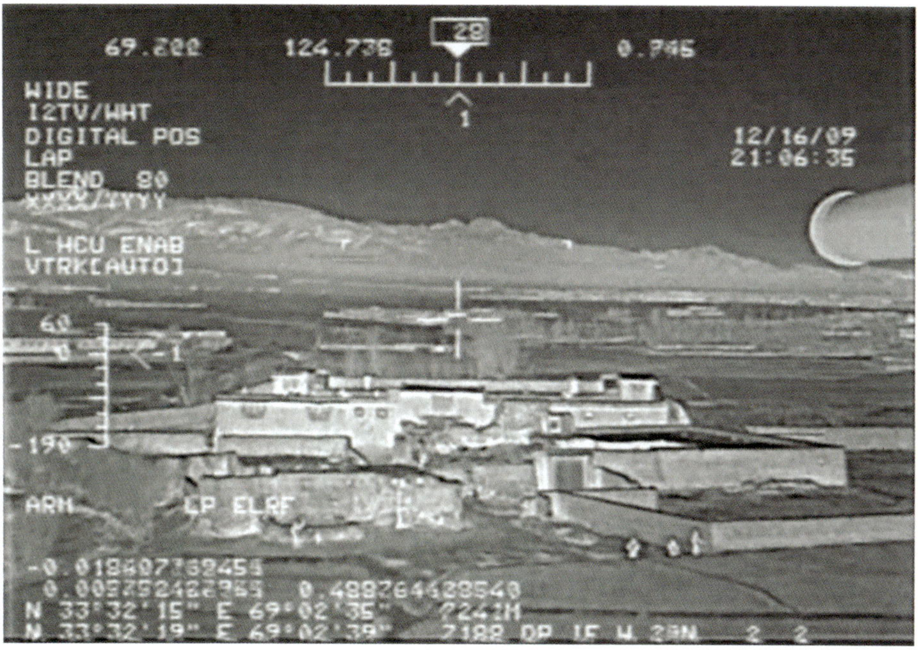

Above: After-action reviews (AARs) often involve reviewing FLIR video recordings, as seen in this image from an MH-47G. (Photo provided by Alan Mack,160th SOAR)

Below: The MH-47 Hover Page provides critical flight information to the pilot in a visually obscured environment during dust/snow landings and low overwater hovering. The display includes power required, barometric and RADAR altitude, speed, and lateral drift trending. Using only this page, the pilot can maintain a stationary hover or desired drift. (Photo provided by Alan Mack, 160th SOAR)

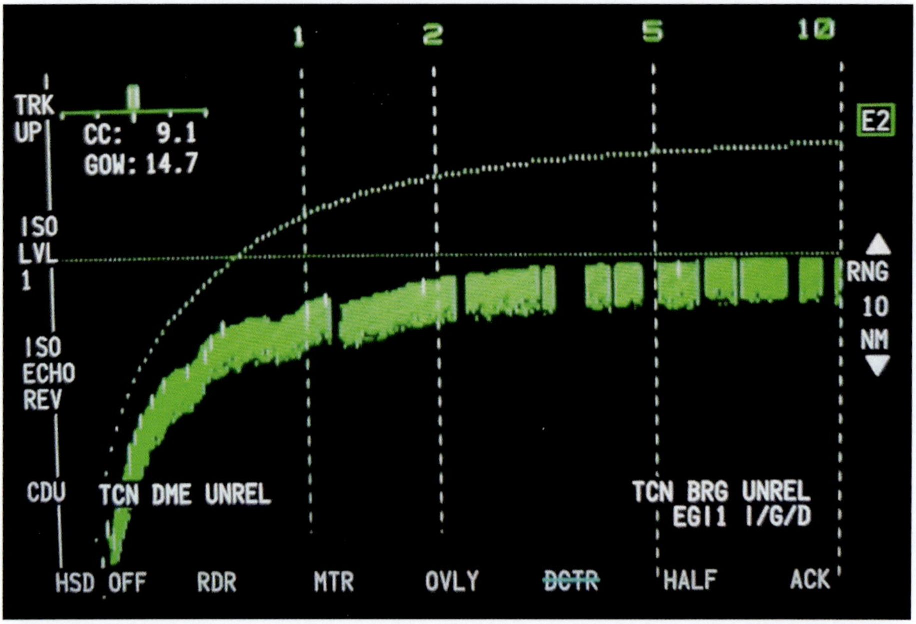

Above: The MH-47 multi-mode radar (MMR) terrain-following (TF) display has multiple configurations. Shown here is an 'E2' page. It depicts a profile view of the terrain the MMR sees for TF commands. The markings use an exponential scale; the thick fuzzy line indicates terrain presence at, 1,2,5, and 10 miles. The dynamic curved-dotted line, referred to as the zero-command line (ZCL), represents the current engine and radar performance. (Photo provided by Alan Mack, 160th SOAR)

Below: Daylight exfils of the assault force are the exception rather than the rule, but sometimes they are required. (Photo provided by 160th SOAR community pool)

Above: Rangers take a knee while waiting for exfil from MH-47. (Photo provided by 160th SOAR community pool)

Below: 2001 – Alan Mack stands outside his burned-out barracks nicknamed 'Motel 6' at Bagram Airbase during the Tora Bora campaign to kill or capture Osama Bin Laden. Relaxed grooming standards and a dirty flight suit are a way of life. (Photo provided by Alan Mack, 160th SOAR)

An MH-47E performs training with Navy SEALS, slinging Special Operations Craft–Riverine (SOC-R) onto Lake Barkley, KY. (Photo provided by Alan Mack, 160th SOAR)

Helicopter air refueling is a skill that requires proficiency due to the proximity of the tanker and receiving aircraft. Here, an MH-47E takes fuel from the left-wing refueling pod of an MC-130. All MH-47 variants can fly indefinitely with additional refuelings, limited only by tanker availability and crew endurance. (Photo provided by Alan Mack, 160th SOAR)

The crew chief in the right cabin door, known as 'Right Gun,' has a clear view of a US Air Force MC-130 tanker. The pilot moves forward to obtain an 'Observation Position' where he will visually verify the condition of the tanker while the entire crew runs through the 'Observation Checklist.' Note the M134' Minigun' in the foreground. (Photo provided by David Burnett, 160th SOAR)

Air refueling from an MC-130 can be challenging, but it can be defined as fun when conditions warrant. This view from the pre-contact position shows the para drogue, hose, and markings leading to the refueling pod. (Photo provided by Alan Mack, 160th SOAR)

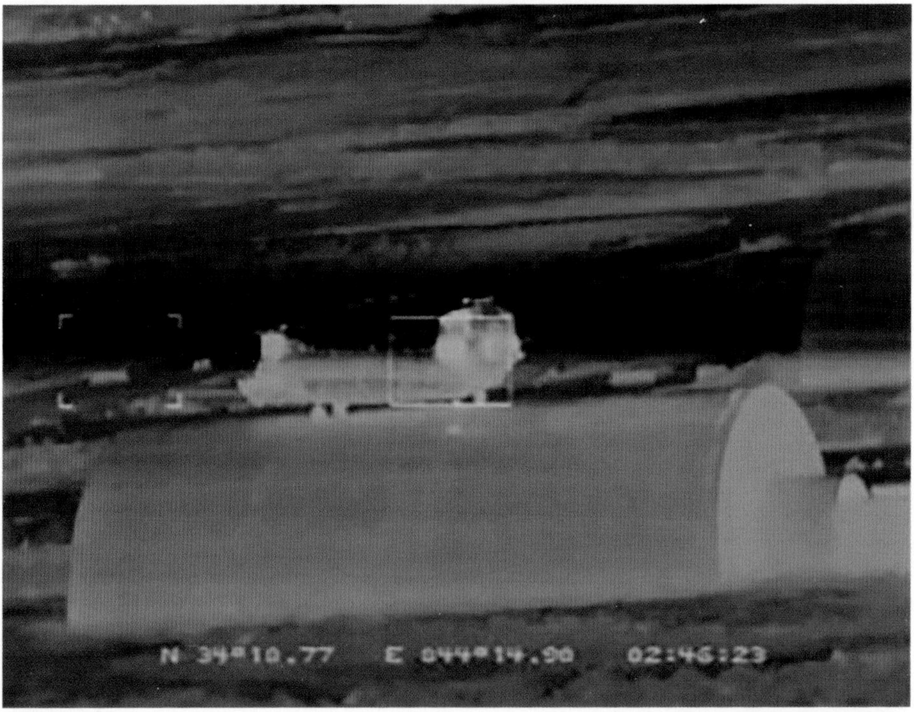

Above: You never know where you'll need to land. An MH-47E, seen here, lands at night atop a Hardened Aircraft Shelter in Iraq. (Photo provided by Alan Mack, 160th SOAR)

Below: Joint Special Operations worldwide sometimes require unique skills, such as refueling in the middle of nowhere. This image shows a 'Wetwing' FARP somewhere in Africa. (Photo provided by Alan Mack, 160th SOAR)

Above: Army and Navy work together using an LHD ship as an Afloat Forward Staging Base (AFSB). Mechanics and Aircrew are working together to get an MH-47 ready for launch. (Photo provided by Dave Ritchie, 160th SOAR)

Below: Maintenance teams at Karshi Khanabad (K2) work around the clock to ensure mission readiness for TF Dagger's MH-47s. Note: A huge dirt berm for security surrounds the area. (Photo provided by Dave Gross, 160th SOAR)

CW5 Alan Mack. (Photo provided by Alan Mack, 160th SOAR)

Practice makes perfect. Here, an MH-47G crew practices the challenging maneuver known as a two-wheel landing in NM. (Photo provided by Boeing Helicopters)

Above: An MH-47D AWC slings a Libyan MI-25 attack helicopter during a clandestine snatch. (Photo provided by Juergen Stark, 160th SOAR)

Below: The 160th operates from Navy vessels with ease. Here, several MH-47Es are parked on an LHD flight deck. (Photo provided by Alan Mack, 160th SOAR)

An MH-47E serves as the backdrop for an after-mission photo op. Task Force aircrews and US Army Rangers capture High Value Target, Objective Kiona in Iraq. (Photo provided by Alan Mack, 160th SOAR)

The center instrument panel of an MH-47G shown here has two backup attitude indicators visible near the top on both sides of the center MFD. Control Data Units (CDU) in the lower corners are data-entry keypads where pilots input radio frequencies, build flight plans, and control Flight Director inputs. (Photo provided by Alan Mack, 160th SOAR)

Above: A successful mission ends with the sun rising on Balad Airbase, Iraq. (Photo provided by Alan Mack, 160th SOAR)

Below: Sunrise after a mission is a welcome sight. Seen here is Cal 'Red Bull' Dockery, whom I mention in the book.

Above: Two MH-47Es from the 160th SOAR fly formation in Southern Korea. (Photo provided by Alan Mack, 160th SOAR)

Below: An MH-47E Fast Ropes ROK SEALS onto a fishing vessel on the high seas. (Photo provided by Alan Mack, 160th SOAR)

Bagram Airbase's living conditions improved dramatically in late 2001. We moved from the burned-out 'Motel Six' into insulated tents with potbelly stoves for heat. The heaters pulled double duty as a cooking surface. Note: Tomato soup warmed in an old coffee can and summer sausage slices sauteed in a saucepan are shown here. (Photo provided by Steve Seaman, 160th SOAR)

level landing area. After storing the location, I scribbled coordinates on my kneeboard and tore it off for Captain Barton to pass to all participants.

Barton coordinated the exfil of Objective Two and a handover of their prisoners, known as PUCs or Persons Under Control, to the intel team. Meanwhile, I informed Thunder Five-Two how I wanted to land in the open desert to crossload our assault package and PUCs. They'd return to Sharana while my single Chinook would assault the new compound, let's call it Objective Three, to keep with this chapter's theme.

The execution of Objective Three went quickly with no friendly losses. Not only did we find all of the targeted individuals among the three Objectives, but we also recovered a treasure trove of computers, human intel, and a gigantic cache of weapons and explosives that we blew in place.

Captain Barton helped coordinate for the F-15Es to drop ordnance on an ammunition storage building, destroying its contents – a successful night by all metrics.

The most meaningful moment was after we returned to parking and shut down. It was a busy mission, to be sure, and I slipped my flight helmet onto the floor and unbuckled my harness when Barton patted me on the shoulder.

"Al, hold on. I want to tell you something."

I turned in my seat to look him in the eyes.

"I thought you were an asshole so many times during training. You challenged me with so many contingencies, and I always thought it was overkill." He paused to collect his words. "But, as hard as you were on me, it pales in comparison to what we just did, and I want to thank you for teaching me all that you have."

Not much compares to that admission. I may have even blushed, but I enjoyed hearing my AMC say that. It shows that the 160th's training is top-notch in all aspects and affirms that humans ARE more important than hardware.

Chapter 9

Humans in SOF Part 1

Many years have passed since I flew a special operations mission in combat, and I'm often asked if I miss it. In some ways, I do. I liked the adventure, adrenaline, purpose, and national pride, but I genuinely miss the people. I miss the camaraderie of facing danger with men I trust with my life, collaborating on solutions to accomplish the impossible, and, best of all, the fun during good times and the humor in the dark times.

Sometimes, the most mundane stories make me smile; for example, I look back to 1998's Operation Desert Fox in Iraq and Kuwait. President Bill Clinton ordered aerial bombardment of Iraq's weapons-of-mass-destruction (WMD) sites to degrade the development of nuclear and chemical munitions. Our mission – perform Personnel Recovery (PR) as needed.

After one week of bombing, President Clinton ordered a pause until roughly a year later, when a similar Operation, Desert Thunder, kicked off. In the meantime, we did not return to the US; instead, we began to support Operation Southern Watch as the primary CSAR and PR platform. Like the previous mission, if someone ejected, bailed out, or crashed, we'd hop in our black Chinooks and race to save them before Iraqi forces could capture or kill survivors.

I've said it before: PR is boring until it's not. Someone else must have a bad day before we put things in motion. Training uses only so much time of the day; the same goes for eating, sleeping, and performing chores. The rest of the time, you watched movies, which in 1998 came as VHS cassettes, not streaming. If someone else was watching, you had to wait your turn and let them finish. The other options were reading a book, playing cards, and competing with peers in sports or other games, such as the handheld Nintendo Gameboy. The Gameboy was approximately the size of a small paperback book. Four AA batteries powered the monochrome grayscale video screen, measuring about 1.8″ x 1.7″. A small speaker or wired headphones provided sound, and a 'head-to-head' cable connected two competing devices for opponents to play directly against one another. The popular game at Ali-Al Salem Airbase in Kuwait was Tetris.

The game revolves around fitting various geometric shapes together as they descend from the top of the video screen. The goal is to create completed horizontal lines without gaps, which then disappear, allowing the player to score points and have more room to work with as he continues to rotate and slide pieces into position. As the game progresses, the shapes fall faster, requiring quick thinking, strategy, and cat-like reflexes. The first player to allow his screen to fill loses.

Now imagine my friend and fellow Flight Lead, Arlo Standish, and me sitting about 2 feet apart in front of a row of tan-colored Air Force Tempur-Tents. Each row of ten tents ran parallel, creating a small tent city; They were long enough to hold twenty beds and had a bunker in between. The formed concrete shelters were intended to protect us during potential air, rocket, or mortar attacks. Arlo and I sat in metal folding chairs beneath a tarp serving as a sunshade, our games tethered for competition.

The daytime temperature hovered around 105 degrees Fahrenheit with no humidity. I wore only black gym shorts and a brown Army T-shirt to compete with Arlo in our intense gaming competition.

Arlo and I furiously tapped at the control keys of our respective Gameboys, each trying to win at any cost. There was no cash prize, trophy, or other tangible item; we played for glory and humiliation or, more accurately, not to be humiliated.

The loser had to stand atop one of the nearby bunkers and loudly proclaim that the winner was the best Tetris player and an all-around better man. Neither of us wanted to give the victor kudos, prestige, or pre-eminence as the camp champion. Still, we would savor our win as if we'd just survived fighting as gladiators in the ancient Roman Coliseum – okay, maybe not, but neither of us wanted to lose.

Game number one was in the books with a win for me.

Arlo complained that the sun was in his eyes, so we traded seats for game number two. The bright sunlight now hindered my vision, and he defeated me in a tense and close match. We moved our seats further under the sunshade with the final game remaining.

I sipped from my water bottle. The previously frozen liquid burned my lips like hot tea left too long on a stove. Arlo and I locked eyes before beginning. "All right, dude, you ready?"

He stared back. "Yup. Hit the button. Let's get this rodeo rolling."

"Go," I announced.

Casual observers who watched the previous two games from a comfortable distance moved closer and watched over our shoulders, cheering softly at first, then louder.

"I've got you," I said as I rotated an 'L' shape into its resting place, and the row disappeared. I looked up briefly to watch Arlo. That was an error in judgment that would cost me the game. I should have continued focusing on the tiny video display as one line after another built steadily toward the top of my screen. I panicked and flubbed another move, sliding a piece when I should have rotated it. The game's music sped up, indicating a soon-to-be finish. The music stopped, and all I could hear was a gentle breeze from the west.

Arlo had won, and I was a loser with a penance to pay.

"Arlo, want to play double or nothing?"

"Nope. I just want to hear how great I am. So get up on that bunker," he said, pointing over his shoulder with his thumb. "Let's hear it."

I set down my game and quickly climbed the concrete structure. It was hot to the touch and covered in dust. "Attention in the tent area. I have vital information to share." I looked to my left and right; there had to be eight Army pilots and easily fifteen Air Force crews standing in a semicircle waiting for my announcement.

"Let's go," Arlo said with his arms crossed.

I cleared my throat and began. "I want everyone in camp to know that Arlo Standish is the best Tetris Player on the continent…"

Arlo interrupted – "And?"

"And he is better than me in every way."

"I can't hear you. Louder, please."

My face was turning red, and it wasn't from sun exposure. I was embarrassed, and dragging this out wasn't making the humiliation any easier. "Arlo Standish is the best Tetris player on the planet, and he beat me fairly and squarely. I can never beat him; he is a better man and pilot than I am."

Applause erupted as Arlo took an exaggerated bow and accepted my praise.

I remember those competitions as vividly as any combat action. Those shared experiences of creativity and camaraderie made miserable conditions fun and somewhat enjoyable – beautiful memories with great people.

Chapter 10

Flight of Five

Afghanistan, Tizni, 2003

In early 2003, American and coalition forces were still shaping the Afghanistan theater of war. Not to be outmaneuvered, the Taliban, Al Qaeda, and the IMU transformed as well. Tactics, techniques, and procedures were morphing and evolving to exploit emerging technologies and experiences for both sides fighting each other.

One thing that didn't change was the violent nature and behavior of the Taliban, particularly in the Kandahar area.

Tizni, a small village 100 miles northwest of Khandhar Airfield, was home to a particularly vicious group terrorizing villagers and Non-Governmental Organization (NGO) relief workers. Our task was to stop their hostile actions and kill or capture the leaders.

Meanwhile, our intelligence analyst, Steve, dropped a target folder on my desk in our planning area and waited for my attention. "What's up, big guy? This looks like a pretty thick package."

"Yes, Sir, we've collected a bunch on these guys. They're a particularly nasty group. On page four of my report, you can see a list of atrocities they committed just this year."

I flipped through the pages. "Who's going to 'action' this Objective?

"It's going to be one of the SF battalions."

"An ODA?"

"No, Sir, an entire battalion of A-Teams."

That was a novel approach that I'd never seen. Five teams, each consisting of twelve Green Berets, would unite and operate as a single element – unique indeed.

+++

The assault force commander, Major Jeff Barley, sat with me for several hours, preparing a concept of operations for Objective Tizni. Not only did we come up with an overall plan, but a robust rehearsal to mitigate the risk associated with this novel method employing SF soldiers. Each ODA normally operated independently, but would now fight as one sixty-man force. My responsibility was to get them to the target, provide casualty evacuation, emergency response, and exfiltration, and return them to Kandahar Airbase.

Major Barley's plan required us to land on the 'X.' Four aircraft would land abeam pre-assigned buildings. One Chinook would orbit nearby with the medical CASEVAC package in case of injury. The mission time window would begin after dark and end with the withdrawal of friendly troops before sunrise.

January nights in Afghanistan are long, therefore the assault force could operate with patience, but we'd need fuel for our Chinooks to enable their lengthy estimated time on target. So I requested a pair of US Air Force MC-130 tankers and an AC-130 for CAS.

The assault was straightforward: five Chinooks flying together until a common release point (RP), then diverging to land at their respective HLZ, with the trail aircraft hanging back at the RP for potential CASEVAC. Once the infil was complete, all five helicopters would fly to the south, hit an aerial refueling track, then ground laager in an open area devoid of structures or known populations to conserve fuel.

I selected points for the air refueling track and a nearby holding area with perimeter security and responsiveness in mind.

The other pilots worked through contingencies and alternate plans for that 'just-in-case' scenario that should never happen but just might. Our crew chiefs worked with the ground force to practice getting on and off the aircraft. They familiarized them with the safety features, weapons systems, ammunition rucks, and, perhaps most importantly, things to avoid touching.

All in all, I was happy with our preparations. We don't always have an opportunity to be so deliberate and thoughtful, but this was one of those rare moments. This mission would require navigating our Chinooks in the dark to a precise point in space to coordinate sequencing and timing so the overhead air platforms didn't tip off the enemy to our pending arrival. Over-the-horizon communications, aerial refueling, CASEVAC, and multiple dust landings were vital components of the mission. Time was available for a rehearsal. We didn't always have an opportunity for a practice run, so I wanted to get the most bang for the buck, and I'd like to think I did.

+++

On my way to brief the crews on how the night's practice would unfold, my commander stopped me in the hallway. "Al, tell me about the rehearsal."

"Yes, Sir, we're going to depart Kandahar as a flight of five, initially heading to the North. We'll test fire the guns and bear left circling the mountain range to the west of Mullah Omar's old headquarters, known as Ghecko."

The Colonel waved his hand in a get-to-the-point motion.

So, I sped up my description using fewer details. "We'll fly through the large terrain saddle just above the compound and drop onto the valley floor, with each Chinook landing to the 'X' abeam the walls with entrance doors. The ground force will assault, and we'll depart to a pre-planned aerial refueling track with an Option-Two tanker formation. Most guys haven't done that since their initial HAR training, so we should knock the cobwebs off."

Colonel Parkinson's frown didn't go unnoticed by me.

"Sir, what's wrong?"

"This whole rehearsal is a waste of time." He sighed as he searched for words that adequately expressed his unhappiness. "You didn't build a mock compound with the exact dimensions as Tizni. You are not flying a similar route, not even close to the time required to get there." He paused again, then kicked his criticism up a notch. "I hear you want to ground laager in the middle of the desert to conserve fuel – no way in hell I'm letting you do that."

My face had to be red. I was pissed and didn't hold back in defense of our plan. "Sir, we don't have time to build a mock-up; the Ground Forces says there's no need. We'll evaluate the landing areas on TOPSCENE (a 3D planning tool similar to today's Google Earth and Street View). HAR with two MC-130s is tricky and needs a run-through; we will test our guns and lasers on the air gunnery range while the ground force does the same with their weapons at Gecko."

Parkinson's facial expression softened somewhat. I hadn't put this together like he would have liked, but he seemed to acknowledge it would suffice. After all, you've probably heard the saying: "Perfect is the enemy of good enough, and good enough is good enough."

He approved my plan with a tiny bit of skepticism and walked into the AMB.

Learn from this – always keep your boss informed and involve him or her in the plan from the outset. After this mission, that lesson served me well for many years in combat, in garrison, and as a civilian.

+++

We flew the rehearsal as planned. The tankers were spot on, the miniguns rocked, the communications 'fills' and over-the-horizon radios worked like a champ, the ground force was happy, and the AC-130 test-fired and 'tweaked' their guns. I was satisfied that we were proficient in every task required for the primary mission and well-versed in alternate courses of action and contingencies. Like I said before, this level of preparation is not often possible, and I was happy. However, I kept in the back of my mind that the weather and the bad guys still had a part to play as potential spoilers. The enemy, as they say, gets a vote.

+++

I woke on mission day around noon and hit the gym for a light workout, followed by a hot shower and breakfast. Based on the time of day, my breakfast wasn't an omelet-to-order, so I settled for a cheeseburger and fries.

I swung through the support offices before meeting with the pilots. I spoke with the tanker navigators, the weather forecaster, the intel NCO, and finally, I had coffee with the ground force commander, Major Barley.

My last stop was Colonel Parkinson's office. "Sir, weather, intel, operations, logistics, the Air Force, the ground force, and our guys are set. What do you say?"

"Al, I think you've prepped everyone, and I'm ready to watch you at work. Let's do this – execute."

Alright, I thought. *Here we go*. "Sir, grab your gear; we're heading to the Chinooks thirty minutes after the update brief."

If it sounds like a deliberate plan is a lot of work, it is.

A time-sensitive target involves much less effort during pre-mission but may be more challenging in the actions-on phase. Consequently, a meticulously planned event can be easier to execute if the extra time is used efficiently to evaluate the threat and consider unconventional angles.

+++

All five MH-47E Chinooks departed the well-lit airfield, and it took a minute to adjust mentally to the lack of illumination beyond Kandahar's perimeter wire. Rolling dunes interspersed with clay-walled compounds stretched as far as I could see.

I adjusted my seat height one notch lower, tweaked my NVGs out of habit, and settled in for a long night as the leader of Maxim flight. Colonel Parkinson sat in the jump seat between and just behind me and my copilot, Jethro. I looked over my right shoulder at the Colonel, who was smiling. Whatever doubts he had earlier seemed gone, and he was enjoying himself, which helped ease my stress. My in-flight chores, like the cruise check, fuel calculations, test fire, lighting adjustments, and intel updates, were behind me. *I must be forgetting something. Maybe I should update the IAS's wind and outside air temperature (OAT).* I nervously scrolled through system pages, looking for anomalies, pending alerts, and engine power calculations that might reveal a power deficit at one of the landing areas – nothing. All was well.

+++

The VWS alarm clock sounded – *Bing Bong – Bing Bong*. I verified the time on my wristwatch, the instrument panel clock, the system time, and the time ahead/time behind, which indicated thirty seconds ahead. Satisfied, I keyed my ICS and announced, "Ten minutes."

The crew and customers acknowledged accordingly, and I checked in with our AC-130. "Hammer One-Three. Maxim Five-One – ten minutes out – checking in as a flight of five MH-47s. Confirm you have products and CONOP for Objective Tizni."

"Maxim Five-One, Hammer copies all and has products. Be advised, the early warning network is quiet, and we will 'burn' the target on your call."

"Hammer, Maxim copies all." I tapped my heel nervously. "Six minutes."

"Six minutes, Aft ready."

"Six minutes, Forward ready."

Jethro followed his steering and speed cues as he climbed a gentle rise. Even in the zero illum, I could make out scrub brush and rocks with no trees to speak of, then the terrain dropped away, and a valley opened up before us. I'd memorized everything about this area from TOPSCENE, satellite imagery, and a thorough map study. I searched for my key landmarks to help identify the series of compounds.

"Maxim Five-One, this is Hammer, target SITREP as follows. One mover with a rifle entered building ten from the north. No other movement seen."

There was no early warning radio traffic, and nobody was walking around the compounds. We've achieved surprise. "Hammer One-Zero, Maxim Five-One, 'Burn' – On."

'Burn' is a pro-word for the AC-130 to illuminate the target with its IR searchlight. It was as if the moon had emerged from the clouds with a focused beam of light only visible through our NVGs.

Jethro hugged a small creek to his right, using it as a handrail straight to our landing area. I was relieved when the cluster of odd-shaped compounds came clearly into view. The main building looked like four long rectangles fused end-to-end; Ours was just beyond it to the east and resembled two trapezoids glued together at the short sides, almost like a bow-tie shape.

"Jethro, that's our landing area to the front."

"Visual, beginning my approach to the ground, hover symbology is selected."

I'd done many missions with my West Virginian copilot, including my first-ever flight into Afghanistan, delivering a team of Green Berets, known as the 'Horse Soldiers', mere weeks after 9/11. Jethro was a good pilot with the rare talent of a great dust landing technique.

"Your altitude is 80 feet. Speed is 42 – looking good."

"Heavy dust mid-cabin, aft gear off 20 feet." The ICS chatter paused only for a long second. "Heavy dust cabin door."

Jethro continued his descent as a thick dust cloud engulfed us. His technique was perfect; as the aft landing gear touched the ground, he lowered the helicopter's nose and applied the brakes.

I keyed my floor mic. "Maxim Five-One is on the ground."

The crew went into action. "Ground contact lights are on, ramp coming down – unloading in progress."

While waiting for an empty aircraft, I leaned toward my CDU and hit the target store button, which recorded our actual landing coordinates and touchdown time for the After Action Review. The dust settled, and I could now make out the compound wall outside our rotor disks. The left minigun had a clear field of fire down the end of the structure, and I'd hate to be an enemy combatant running around the far corner because my left gunner would cut him in half. But nobody came out, instead barricading themselves for the close-quarters fight and an explosive breach soon to come.

Time to go. "Before Takeoff is complete, clear up left and right."

"Aft ready – cleared for flight."

"Forward ready – cleared for flight."

"Maxim Five-One coming out." Jethro focused on the hover page and applied power, eventually clearing the sixty-foot-tall dust cloud.

"Jethro, you're clear to accelerate."

"Copy, Right Seat is accelerating."

"Maxim Five-One is clear of the cloud and accelerating to 80 knots airspeed – heading one-eight-zero – 300 feet AGL."

I listened to the flight's internal radio frequency and counted each chalk's call, clearing the dust. The next pro-word I wanted to hear was 'Turkey,' indicating a chalk had rejoined the flight.

"Five-Two – Turkey."

"Five–Three–Turkey," and so on.

Jethro sped up to 130 knots toward our tankers when we had all five. The infil was flawless, and we were headed for fuel, though I was concerned about the latest radio call: "Shots fired on the Objective."

CASEVAC for an injured assaulter could come at any moment.

+++

Helicopter Aerial Refueling (HAR) can be complex, but the tried and true procedures are sound. A special operations variant of the trusty C-130 Hercules outfitted with a refueling pod suspended beneath each wing, will rendezvous in the air with its receivers, in this case, us.

The aerial link-up occurs on a preplanned path creatively called a HAR Track. The track begins at the Initial Point (IP), where the receiver crosses at the join-up altitude, air refueling speed, and heading to cross the Control Point (CP) at the Control Time (CT).

In the meantime, the tanker is approaching at 240 knots from the opposite direction, offset one-half mile to the left and flying 300 feet higher.

The two airborne elements will eventually converge at the CP and pass gas together *(Yes, that phrase still gets a chuckle out of pilots like a bad dad joke).*

I opened my handy HAR checklist and began to read the challenge and response.

"Okay, guys, let's run the rendezvous checklist. The HAR frequency is set in the number two radio – 287.5 secure – TACAN is Five-One Yankee, air-to-air." When I entered that channel in the CDU, the distance between us and the tankers showed on our MFDs. "Tanker is at 30 miles and closing," I announced.

The tanker, callsign Papa One-One, as if on cue, passed a mutual altimeter setting to ensure we had a shared understanding of altitudes. "Maxim Five-One, Papa One-One – Altimeter 30.01."

"30.01, I replied."

I began to read aloud:

"Type of Rendezvous – Receiver Low."
"Join up altitude – 5,700 MSL."
"Refueling altitude – 6,000."
"Refueling airspeed – 115 knots."
"Tanker Callsign – Papa One-One and Papa One-Two."

Typically, we'd only utilize one MC-130, but the five of us needed more gas than one tanker could pass, so the Air Force provided us with an Option-Two formation. The tankers maintained a 2-mile separation while we split our flight into two elements. Maxims Five-One, Five-Two, and Five-Three stayed on the lead tanker while Five-Four and Five-Five backed away from us and joined the second tanker. Once refueled, we'd close up our flight distance and reassume formation as a flight of five.

After completing the Rendezvous checklist, I ticked off the steps in the join-up checklist.

My crew chief advised me of the tanker's location. "Sir, the tanker is turning left at six o'clock."

I could tell this tanker pilot was good. He dissipated his speed as he came around from our left, passing our backside, and slowly moved past our right door slightly above us, stopping relative motion to our right front.

"Tanker is at two o'clock," Jethro announced, then he gently climbed to join Papa One-One; Chalks two and three followed.

Once in position, I finished the last checks and equipment adjustments and waited for a green signal light from the port-side jump door. The green light, looking like a traffic signal at a road intersection, flashed for two seconds and disappeared.

"There's our signal to move to the pre-contact position and for Five-Three to cross over to the right wing; Five-Two will stay on the left with us."

Jethro made a deliberate movement down and right until we were behind the left wing of the MC-130, where a long black hose trailed from a hydraulic spool in the left refueling pod. At the end of the hose was a white silk forty-six-inch wide donut-shaped para-drogue with tapered aluminum struts. The 'turkey feathers,' as they're known, ran from the silk donut to a spring-loaded coupler, creating a cone shape with the large opening facing us.

Our blades were 30 feet long, and the refueling probe extended about 25 feet in front of the helicopter's nose on the right side of the cockpit. Jethro maneuvered to maintain our refuel probe tip about 10 feet away, keeping the drogue out from under our forward rotor.

I reached the HAR light panel on the center console between Jethro and me and flipped it on. A horizontal IR beam of light illuminated the root of the left wing, needing only a slight movement to the left, which I did. Now, Jethro could use the entire wing length, flaps, and fuel dump tubes as visual cues. The white hose markings and refueling range were clearly visible, making it easy to see that conditions were excellent for HAR.

"Alright, Jethro, I think you're good. How about you?"

"Al, cues are good; I'm in position – movement to contact." He moved the cyclic forward while simultaneously adding power with the Thrust, and we accelerated ever-so-slightly. The drogue remained steady, and our probe tip entered the silk circle, brushing along the tapered Turkey feathers. His forward movement and the cone shape guided the tip until it hit the coupler, which clamped the tip with a roller assembly held inward by spring pressure. It would take about 420 pounds of rearward pull to disengage from the drogue assembly.

Once connected, he eased up and left, away from the MC-130 fuselage, until he was level with the wing. The hose drooped in a mild arc, causing it to rest at the lower left portion of the pod opening. Then, with mild flight control adjustments, he'd maintain the refueling markings in their proper range.

"Sir, we're taking fuel."

"Roger. Go ahead and take 6,000 pounds. We're going to do this two more times tonight."

Five minutes later, we had enough fuel for the next phase of our operation.

"Okay, let's disengage and let Chalk Three on the hose." But before we disconnected, I reached overhead to the IR position light switch. I flashed it three times, indicating we would back up and pass behind Maxim Five-Two, allowing him to duplicate our actions. Once he finished, he backed away from the hose and rejoined to my left before Five-Three crossed back to our side of the MC-130.

Once we were a flight of three again, we descended to 300 feet AGL, maintaining course while awaiting Chalks Four and Five to accelerate away from their tanker and join us.

+++

We orbited with our fuel tanks sufficiently full, waiting for a CASEVAC or exfil call. But as I looked around, I could see no sign of cultural buildup, no farms – nothing – just a large flat valley. The colonel noticed me searching the area and marking my map.

"Al, you may be on to something. I think this area is suitable for your ground laager plan. I approve. Go ahead and give it a shot."

"Yes, Sir," I said as I prepared to issue orders to the other pilots. "Flight, this is Five-One; prepare to land in a herringbone pattern using my heading of three-six-zero as the base."

Each chalk acknowledged and alternated their landing headings. Chalk Two landed behind me on a magnetic heading of three-three-zero, and Chalk Three landed behind him, facing to my right on a zero-three-zero heading. With each helicopter landing one at a time, the subsequent landing directions were easy to pick out. Chalk four landed three-zero-zero, and five touched down, heading zero-six-zero. This herringbone pattern allowed each set of miniguns to cover specific fields of fire without hitting the helicopter to their front or rear. If we detected anybody approaching, we'd simply depart and orbit somewhere else.

We were far enough away from Tizni that I couldn't reach the ground force with a line-of-sight radio, so I contacted the AC-130 overhead. "Hammer One-Zero, Maxim Five-One, be advised we are holding on the ground at grid 41S PR 54962 61491 and are a twenty-minute flight away. Please relay that information to the ground force and provide a SITREP when able."

"Maxim, Hammer copies all." After a slight delay, the AC-130 got back to me. "Words passed, and SITREP follows. Buildings ten, three, four, and seven are secure. Building eleven has at least three military-aged males barricaded with a PKM and grenades – attempting a callout at this time."

Time was on our side as long as we had fuel. We'd hit the tankers again when our fuel got to 3,000 pounds and then repeat as long as the assaulters needed it, the fuel held out, or the sun rose.

+++

A long night was coming to an end when the exfil request came across the SATCOM. I yawned as I wrote the exfil request on my kneeboard. I scribbled the coordinates, landing headings, and the Eagle count. Everyone was coming out on the helicopter they rode in, but fifteen Military-Aged-Males (MAMs) were being detained and coming off the objective spread across the entire flight.

So, we returned to Tizni, 'cleaned the PZ,' and returned to Kandahar. No friendlies were injured, the targeted individuals were either killed or captured, and reams of papers and several computers ripe for exploitation came off target.

The concept of the operation, rehearsals, terrain evaluation, and many other aspects of mission planning and execution were etched in my mind for future use. Much like I learned from my shootdown in 2002, I gained experience coordinating and influencing assets to my advantage. I can relate this experience to the foundation for how I later planned and flew during the successful rescue of Lone Survivor, Navy SEAL Marcus Luttrell, as described in my first book, *Razor 03, A Night Stalker's Wars*.

Chapter 11

Mount Hope III

1988

If my segmented rehearsal for Objective Tizni was helpful, it wasn't the only way to prepare for an operation. One of the best full-blown rehearsals dates back to the earliest days of the 160th. The organization was not regimental-sized in 1987 but was known as the 160th Special Operations Aviation Group (SOAG), commanded by Colonel John 'Coach' Dailey. I was privileged to discuss Operation Mount Hope III with him and CW4 Juergen Stark (RIP), the Flight Lead.

First, I need to explain the situation in Chad during the 1987 'Toyota War,' which was so named because all participants used Toyota Hilux pickup trucks and Toyota Land Cruisers as technical war vehicles. The war took place in Northern Chad on the Libyan border, resulting in a stinging defeat for Soviet ally Muammar Gaddafi. His forces suffered tremendous losses of men and equipment, primarily due to battle, but much of it was abandoned in retreat.

With the Cold War still raging between the USSR and the United States, Libya's exported Soviet armor, air defense missile systems, and aircraft left intact on the battlefield were potential treasures if retrieved. A Libyan MI-25 HIND attack helicopter was particularly interesting at the abandoned military airfield at Ouadi Doum. The export variant of the vaunted MI-24 sat on a dusty tarmac with damaged engines, unable to fly under its own power. Two efforts to retrieve the coveted helicopter failed, forcing planners back to the drawing board.

Operational security was a vital component of the new plan – an airlift.

If the Libyans got wind of another attempt to abscond with their stricken aircraft, they'd likely send a fighter aircraft to blow it in place to keep it out of Western hands. A Chinook was the only US helicopter capable of lifting the heavy gunship, flying the required distance from friendly territory into the semi-permissive environment, and returning to permissive territory.

The problem of getting a Chinook within range and light enough to carry the heavy load was theoretically possible but improbable.

+++

Colonel Dailey called his best Flight Lead into his office.

CW4 Juergen Stark had been with the 160th since its inception and was probably the most experienced Chinook pilot in the Group. He accepted the mission to fly into Chad and steal the HIND using MH-47 Chinooks as the lift platform. "That damn HIND was fricken heavy," he told me. It weighed over 18,000 lbs empty but needed to get down to 16,500 lbs for him to lift and carry the attack bird into permissive territory. So, he and his fellow planners started figuring out how to get the weight down for transport, rigging the cargo slings, fuel requirements, navigating and communicating over the horizon, and other associated tasks.

Juergen figured the planning team would solve the math problems involving distances, weights, and times, but he still needed to find a suitable Forward Support Base (FSB) and figure out how to get his Chinooks there. He could fly to an aircraft carrier or other air-capable navy ship. He ruled out self-deployment, though theoretically possible. Both of these methods would work, but they lacked flexibility in timing and required massive external support, which would strain OPSEC.

Air transport was the best option. A US Air Force C-5 Galaxy would be ideal, but no established load plans existed for such a tactical movement. New procedures and equipment had to be developed, and the 160th was up to the task.

Ironically, the man attributed with inventing the now-established procedures for transporting MH-47 helicopters in Air Force transports once served in the US Army Air Corps in Libya, the very same country from which they were now trying to acquire the armed helicopter. His imagination and engineering skills produced wheeled ground support equipment capable of carrying a single Chinook's forward and aft transmission and one for the Aft pylon. Rotor blades would fit in a blade rack inside the cargo compartment of the helicopter, and a small tactical crane known as a SCAMP would be used to disassemble and reassemble components needed to fit inside the C-5. Ultimately, the load plan consisted of two MH-47 Chinooks, the SCAMP, and twenty-five crew and mechanics fitting into a single Galaxy. The timeline for teardown and buildup was then and is still classified. Needless to say, it was impressive then and is much quicker now with the technology of our times.

With the method of transport settled, N'Djamena International Airport in Southwestern Chad became the planned FSB. Now, Juergen had to convince Colonel Dailey that his plan could work.

Carrying an aircraft of any type using slings below a Chinook can be a challenge, as the cargo in question has aerodynamic properties that, when used for flying, are desirable, but as a sling load can bring about catastrophic results if the cargo gains lift in flight.

The maintenance team continued to refine the air transport equipment and had to get creative with the rigging procedure. Without an actual HIND, the next best airframe to practice with was a US Navy SH-3 Sea King, the military version of the Sikorsky S-61.

A remote training compound at Fort Bragg, NC, was a quiet and isolated location where the team could experiment with slings and harnesses. First, the experienced airborne riggers from Fort Bragg looked at the airframe and decided not to 'hang test' the analog under a crane because they couldn't get one without drawing attention to their activities. The team of riggers was sure they could match parameters with simple math and a little artistic flair. They inserted 500 pounds of steel plates in various airframe sections to match the HIND's weight. Then they sorted through their harnesses to develop suitable straps to ensure the load would ride properly under a Chinook.

Once convinced the helicopter would ride properly, they moved on to flight testing and slung it beneath an MH-47D and flew at ever faster test speeds, eventually reaching 130 knots.

Colonel Dailey received Juergen's progress update and asked him to prove that two MH-47Ds could deploy by C-5, be built up in an austere environment, fly 500 NM, and pick up a sling-loaded HIND. Then, they still had to return the same distance, tear down, reload the C-5s, and return with their precious cargo to the United States.

+++

Roswell, New Mexico, simulated the FSB at N'Djamena roughly thirty days before mission execution. An Air Force C-5 delivered two MH-47s and associated personnel under the cover of darkness to an isolated and austere airstrip in the middle of the American Southwest. By the time the sun went down, the two Chinooks had taken off into the dark and were configured with internal fuel tanks, enabling a 500-mile circuitous route to Biggs Army Airfield in El Paso, TX. Four hours and ten minutes of flying with NVGs brought them within sight of their destination.

Five 500-gallon rubber fuel blivets were waiting for them, weighing 16,500 lbs, the expected weight of the abandoned HIND. Although Juergen was the Flight Lead, the trail aircraft would be the primary lift bird. Juergen would navigate and occasionally fly around Chalk Two to visually check out the load and verify it rode smoothly. If not, the valuable cargo might need to be jettisoned in the interest of safety.

Only one of the two planned fuel stops along the return route was needed. Not only did Juergen change his NVG batteries in flight, but his favorite snack sat comfortably in his flight suit's right leg pocket – peanut M&Ms. He was infamous in the Night Stalkers for his love of the candy-coated yummies, which he shared with his fellow pilots as he watched the successful loading of his two Chinooks. Everyone reboarded and flew back to Fort Campbell with a successful rehearsal and proof-of-concept.

Now, they just had to wait for approval to execute the actual mission, which might never happen due to interservice rivalries and concerns from the US State Department. Colonel Dailey argued for the mission to go while he was in the Middle East, checking on another 160th mission – Operation Prime Chance.

Juergen knew that the odds were against the Department of Defense allowing him to fly into Chad, even though the French government received permission on behalf of the Americans. But to his surprise, in mid-May 1988, the Execute Order (EXORD) came through, and the teardown of the two MH-47Ds began in earnest. Within a few hours, two C-5s arrived at Fort Campbell, KY, and departed quickly for Africa. Once on the ground at N'Djamena International Airport, the maintenance team put the two Chinooks back together in record time.

Colonel Dailey repositioned from the Persian Gulf to join the Chinook crews as the Air Mission Commander. He arrived in time to be brought up to speed and get a hot meal. The food wasn't hot because of professional kitchen prep, but because it sat out in temperatures exceeding 100 degrees Fahrenheit for an extended time, causing some digestive and intestinal challenges for some crewmembers. Unfortunately for some, they had to push on with whatever discomfort they felt, and the mission proceeded with a midnight launch to the north.

Juergen took the lead and accelerated to his maximum range airspeed of 135 knots. His Flight Engineer immediately began transferring fuel from the internal tank to the main fuel system. It was better to know early if the notoriously fragile tank pumps would function properly. If not, the helicopters could turn around, fix the problem, and potentially continue the mission during the same cycle of darkness.

Navigation systems of the day were rudimentary and primitive by today's standards. Juergen held a map on his lap while following a wind-adjusted heading. There weren't many terrain or man-made features to follow, so his navigator, another pilot sitting at the left front cabin, typically a gunner's position, toyed with a Tracor OMEGA and a Doppler Navigation system to help keep the flight on track. The flight would last almost five hours, with fuel being a valuable commodity; even a few degrees of heading or track error could put them several miles off course with little fuel reserve to play with.

The lead Chinook was a more advanced version of the Delta model, known as an AWC, or Adverse Weather Cockpit. Chalk Two was a 'Warbird,' as they called it, with nothing unique or modified other than some secure radios not found on a CH-47D. Mounted under the aircraft's nose was a thermal camera. The FLIR used differential temperatures in the infrared spectrum, and the desert at night produced a crisp video to help the pilots avoid terrain and obstacles that might be difficult to see using only NVGs.

Juergen played with the FLIR settings to achieve the best possible video because there seemed to be an odd cluster of heat ahead, appearing as a white-hot blob on his display. "I'm fricking doing something wrong," he said to his copilot. While zooming in, he started to laugh. The heat source was a herd of camels. His low-flying aircraft passed close enough to see individual faces on the display.

Temperatures in the desert typically drop off dramatically, but it was still over 100 degrees Fahrenheit, and dehydration could sneak up without drinking enough water. The crew commented on the plastic bottles burning their lips and being hot enough to make tea, but as Juergen, a man not known for complaining, told me, "It was wet."

The four-and-a-half-hour flight passed, and the crew scanned the horizon as they approached the target area. The airfield and HIND were nowhere in sight. The navigator re-examined his notes and map markings. As near as he could tell, they had to be within at least 5 miles. Juergen keyed the HF radio and announced the execution checklist call for arrival in the area, but not the pro-word for arriving at the actual airfield. He began ever-expanding counterclockwise orbits in search of their destination. Chalk Two offset and mirrored those orbits, but in a clockwise manner to cover more ground. Within three orbits, the HIND appeared in Lead's FLIR. Colonel Dailey, quietly observing from the jump seat, noticed it first.

The two Chinooks landed separately on the airport parking ramp next to the crippled Soviet gunship.

As their rotors coasted to a stop, Juergen's crew downloaded the external fuel tanks from both MH-47s while Chalk Two's crew checked the partially sand-covered HIND. A C-130 alerted by Juergen's execution checklist call arrived with a support team. The same riggers who performed the Fort Bragg harness test began rigging the slings. The C-130 had a dual purpose; one was to bring the riggers and hookup team, and the second was to transport the now-removed internal fuel tanks, the HIND rotor blades, rocket pods, and extraneous gear, so the Chinooks had to only worry about carrying the HIND.

Juergen looked at his wristwatch and then toward the east, watching as the sun started to creep skyward. It was hot and would soon be hotter.

+++

The crew finished the prep work in less than an hour, and it was time to go. The C-130 would depart last, taking the sling hookup men and head south, accelerating ahead of the Chinooks to set up a tactical WETWING FARP for the first fuel stop at Faya-Largeau. Juergen took off and orbited the lift bird; his FLIR locked on the HIND for video recording.

Chalk Two picked up to a hover above the load; a heavy dust cloud roiled up by rotor wash made visibility tricky, but being a daylight flight, the crew could still see the ground through the thick obscuration.

Juergen watched patiently as the Chinook's blades coned under load. "That Bitch is fricking heavy," he said over the radio.

"Yes, it is," said Chalk Two. "I figure she weighs about 18,000 lbs."

That was far heavier than they'd planned for, but they'd come too far now to stop. The MH47 was powerful enough, but it would need some maintenance when it returned home. Juergen looked at Colonel Dailey, who remained quiet in the Jump Seat, giving a thumbs-up to continue the mission.

Juergen announced on the HF that they were en route to the first fuel stop, and off they went with no problems on the first leg of their return journey. They took fuel from the C-130 and worked their way back into the air. Life was about to get more interesting as they raced toward their next fuel stop at a French Foreign Legion base in Moussoro.

Chalk Two set the HIND on a prepared surface amid a light dust cloud, shut down, and refueled first, followed by Lead.

Juergen noticed the wind picking up. There was no windsock, but he estimated the wind to be around 20 knots and gusting to 40 or 50 knots. He thought he saw a hint of sand in the air to the northwest. If they were lucky, this would be as bad as the weather would get, but more than likely, a nasty sandstorm would engulf them before they arrived at N'Djamena.

A quick repeat of their previous two hookups and departures ensued as they entered the final 120 miles of their flight route. Juergen was glad they made a quick turn on the ground because they might still be able to outrun the sandstorm his crew chief could see closing from behind.

Chalk Two's ride in the turbulent air caused a dangerous oscillation in the slung HIND, and it flew upward with a near miss at the bottom of the Chinook. The crew chief was a fraction of a second from jettisoning the load to avoid collision. Instead, they slowed to 100 knots and banked the aircraft gently, thus stabilizing the load. The downside to a slower but smoother ride was that the rapidly nearing storm would definitely catch the two MH-47s.

They continued at the reduced speed, taking longer to arrive at their destination and consuming more fuel. Juergen did the fuel consumption math in his head as he popped a handful of warm peanut M&Ms into his mouth. A smiling Colonel Dailey tapped him on the shoulder and held out his hand for the semi-melting candies. "It melts in your mouth, not in your hands – bullshit," Juergen said as he slid the yellow bag out of his leg pocket and handed it to his boss.

The pilots stayed on their intended course as the storm caught up during the final 5 miles. Juergen could barely make out the airport just ahead. The thick dust cloud made flying and navigating much more difficult. However, he made a final course adjustment that allowed both aircraft to sit down beside their waiting C-5s just as the storm intensified for another hour or so.

Once the weather settled down, the maintenance team went into action, partially disassembling the MH-47s, loading them according to the manifest, and preparing for departure. Juergen conducted a post-flight inspection on his Chinook. The sandstorm had blasted most of the fuselage paint to bare metal or primer. All six rotor blades had extreme damage to the leading edge due to sand erosion, as did the first stage of his turbine engine blades. He wondered how long they could have flown before engine problems ended their flight prematurely. He looked toward the sky, thanking God he didn't have to find out.

In the meantime, another team loaded the HIND on the second C-5. Once loaded, the two heavily laden cargo aircraft headed for the Ascension Islands to refuel and reset. After a minor maintenance delay with one of the C-5s, they resumed their return trip to Fort Campbell, KY.

The HIND ended up at Fort Rucker's Test Activity, where it was evaluated, analyzed, restored, and flown for many years.

Juergen and Colonel (now Brigadier General) Dailey fondly told me that the entire mission, from C-5 landing in Chad to mission execution and departing with the stolen HIND, took only 66 hours.

Operation Mount Hope III was the first real-world use of MH-47s, demonstrating the 160th Chinooks' global reach.

Chapter 12

Flight Lead

The US Secretary of Defense, Donald Rumsfeld, ordered my first combat mission into Afghanistan. So, besides a Commander in the 160th, there is arguably no more critical role than the Flight Lead. Typically, a senior Warrant Officer analyzes the mission and develops the air mission's primary course of action and alternatives. He coordinates the fire support plan and contingencies with the ground force commander. The Flight Lead briefs the commander, coordinates staff support, and presents the air mission brief (AMB). He is the flight leader and primary navigator responsible for executing the air mission, including any pre-planned first-level contingencies that may occur. That's a lot of words to say; the Flight Lead accepts a mission and intent from the Commander, comes up with the plan, tells everyone else what they're doing, and then leads a flight of Night Stalkers to their target on time, plus or minus thirty seconds.

Regarding career timelines, the time it takes to achieve Flight Lead status varies among airframe series (MH-60, MH-6, and MH-47). Skill and talent are the basis for the position; add the extent of experience and exposure to training or real-world operations, and you may be eligible for an evaluation. A Fully Mission Qualified (FMQ) pilot might get a look in the Regiment as early as five years.

My favorite Flight Lead evaluation that I administered occurred in Korea during the spring of 2005. CW2 Jasper Freed, aka Jethro, had been in the thick of many fights since the attacks of 9/11. He'd demonstrated superior flying skills, critical thinking, and the ability to stay calm and make good decisions under enemy fire, in bad weather, or other high-pressure situations.

As the Regimental MH-47 Standardization Instructor Pilot (SIP), I was responsible for evaluating and certifying Jethro as a Flight Lead. Getting through one of my check rides was no easy task, and I would probably be more brutal to Jethro, ironically, because of my affection for him.

Before I met him as a pilot, he'd been an MH-47 Flight Engineer for several years before attending Warrant Officer Flight Training and returning to the Regiment as a Chinook Pilot. I liked everything about the big West Virginian. He stood 6′2″ and weighed in around 230 pounds. He was a natural at flying and, more importantly, laughed at my jokes.

I signed him off as an FMQ in early 2000, and together we deployed to Task Force Dagger in 2001. I chose him as my copilot in Razor 03 as we infiltrated enemy lines to deliver SF ODA 595, informally known as the 'Horse Soldiers.'

Now, four years later, I had mixed emotions. Progressing Jethro to Flight Lead was bittersweet for me. On the one hand, I was proud to watch him move to the pinnacle of a Night Stalker's peer group, and on the other, it meant I'd never fly with him again as a crew. He'd have his own flight to lead. I knew he was up to the task and wanted to share my experiences and life-saving tips throughout the evaluation scenario.

+++

Gimpo International Airport was well-lit, and the air conditioning was chilly. I bent at the hips and side to side, then stretched my calves while leaning against a vertical support. The flight from Fort Campbell to Seoul, Korea, was long but smooth. I flew to Seattle for a short visit with our 4th Battalion Chinook unit, then proceeded with a roughly 20-hour flight to Korea. I should have slept, but couldn't get comfortable, nor did my thoughts quiet down long enough to nap. I was mulling over the planned scenario for Jethro's Flight Lead evaluation, but it didn't strike me as comprehensive enough, and I considered improving the scenario.

My experience in the Global War on Terror made me a self-identified (in my own mind) expert on planning missions. Still, managing Special Operators' personalities and expectations was the real talent of the Flight Lead. Natural talent is essential, but convincing the assault force to do what you want them to do, while making them believe the idea is theirs, is the real skill. I intended for Jethro to demonstrate his ability to lead, and I would mentor him along the way, maybe saving him heartache in the real world, as they say, by 'bleeding in training.'

My leg muscles were still tight when my good friend Achmed walked up wearing a green one-piece flight suit. "Al, I'm Glad to see you made it."

"Achmed, how's it…"

His bear hug stopped me mid-sentence. Achmed's nickname came from his Middle Eastern, or was it a Mediterranean, or maybe Hispanic complexion? He always played up his ethnic appearance as it suited him. "Al, follow me. Let's get your bags. I've got a helicopter waiting to take us to Daegu."

I thought he was kidding, but sure enough, he led me out a security door, where a freshly painted, flat-black MH-47E sat.

She sure looks pretty, I thought, and I climbed aboard for an hour's flight to Daegu Airbase.

While en route, Achmed explained our slight quandary. Due to wartime deployments and maintenance, only two MH-47 Chinooks were available. However, the complexity of using multiple and disparate airframes is a crucial component of any Flight Lead evaluation. If the FLQ candidate has only one type of aircraft performance metric, it's too simple; any FMQ can handle that. We needed more problems to solve, and we got them with the help of conventional units – remember SOF Truth number five: most Special Operations require non-SOF assistance.

The operational planners behind Jethro's evaluation were creative and diligent. They scooped up willing participants such as ROK SEALS, ROK Rangers, US SF Green Berets, AH-64 Apaches, CH-47D Chinooks, a pair of MC-130 tankers, and associated contract waterborne vessels.

The evaluation concept was simple: Task Force Cougar would stand up at the Korean military base in Daegu starting Monday, April 10, 2005. Once forces assembled, familiarization flights and rehearsals would take effect for a deliberate mission, followed by an in-extremis or Time-Sensitive Target (TST). Jethro's challenge, in this case, wasn't just a math problem but competing procedures with SOF vs. Conventional units. He needed to operate safely at night with units that had never flown together.

I sat down with him and his Air Mission Commander, a young Captain still new to the 160th. "Jethro, here's your target. It's a cargo ship that will transit the southern coast of Korea near Busan." I placed a photograph of the ship in front of him. "We will get updates on the boat's location and timing using national assets."

"What am I doing with the ship?"

"You're going to Fast Rope ROK SEALS onto the deck so they can rescue a kidnapped Korean diplomat en route to a small bayside compound. The North Korean spies transporting him will drive him to the port of Yangiam for final transport to Pyongyang." I paused to let him finish writing what I'd just told him.

Jethro leaned back in his chair as he pulled a can of dip from his arm pocket, tapped the can lightly, then took a pinch of the finely chopped tobacco and placed it between his cheek and gums. "Al, do you have an Earliest Anticipated Launch Time (EALT)?"

"Yup. I'd say you've got at least three days to get ready. Oh, and you'll be using the AH-64s with their Longbow radars to find and fix the ship. They'll also provide gun support in a pinch. You'll use the CH-47s from Camp Humphries to lift ROK Rangers to the destination port. They'll lock down the ship he's headed to." I started to get up from the table, but paused. "I want you and Captain Kidd to back-brief me tomorrow on how you plan to integrate your conventional forces and provide me with three COAs."

"Roger that," was all he said.

+++

Jethro sat down with the conventional pilots to explain how the 160th customarily did business. He wanted to know if they could operate that way or if he needed to modify any procedures to accommodate them. Nobody voiced any concerns; they were excited to try our ways.

You've heard of the process of Crawl–Walk–Run. That's how Jethro approached the operation. The first thing he wanted was to be able to communicate, but there were some minor challenges there. All the airframes had FM, UHF, and VHF radios, but the conventional helicopters could only talk securely on their FM radio. The MH-47Es could securely speak on all three line-of-sight radios and had HF and SATCOM radios for over-the-horizon communications. The AH-64 Longbows had a sophisticated target handoff system, incompatible with the other helicopters, and could only work between the Apaches.

One secure radio was sufficient for inter-flight communications. If enemies picked up or intercepted transmissions, they'd know someone was near, but they couldn't decipher the electronically ciphered conversations.

The UHF radio would be helpful as an in-the-clear backup for inter-flight and a get-well or safety frequency.

Air Traffic Control frequencies operate between 118.0 and 137.0 MHz, so the VHF radio was suitable. The remaining radios were a bonus.

It's been said that good communication and fuel are all that's needed to complete a mission successfully; Jethro intended to prove that.

+++

Once everyone was comfortable with standard radio phraseology and how the Task Force could and would talk, Jethro arranged for introductory daylight rehearsal flights. These over-simplified flights would form the building blocks of a more comprehensive and complex mission.

Jethro led the flight of six helicopters around the airbase traffic pattern with stop-and-go approaches. Once convinced everyone was comfortable, he departed the pattern and headed toward the south, intending to fly low level and then terrain flight into and around the surrounding mountains. He practiced several formation flight maneuvers and adjustments before returning to base, eating chow, and repeating the entire process after dark using Night Vision Goggles. These extended hours felt like a flight school refresher, but everyone agreed the time was worth the effort.

The next day involved intelligence briefings discussing the targeted area, the enemy's likely reactions, and their most deadly responses to our presence. Jethro devised an elaborate plan that would typically have been simple to accomplish with only special operations aircrews. Still, the dissimilar mix of airframes and conventional crews could be a challenge. I've met many pilots who claim they could be in the 160th, but they don't try for whatever reason. I closely watched the crews assembled. It turns out they all volunteered for this operation and, in my opinion, were more than capable. We even got a few to join us when they completed their Korea tour.

Jethro scheduled another rehearsal to practice the actual mission, not just airmanship. I selected an area similar to where the hostage rescue would occur and passed it along to the AMC, who looked down his nose at my choices. He wanted to use another place of his choosing. Now, I must explain that although he is technically responsible for the overall success of the air mission, the Flight Lead's responsibility is similar to how a conductor leads an orchestra. The mission is already written and blessed by the commander and Air Mission Commander, then the Flight Lead sets the tempo, cues actions, and navigates to his target. The AMC is usually much more of an advisor than a leader, although in some cases, he may play a more prominent role because of his experience. In this case, our young captain wanted to be more involved, and it was getting in the way of how I wanted to evaluate Jethro. At some point, I'd have to make him stop showing me how much he knew so I could focus on what my candidate did. For now, I'd just let things play out.

Jethro's rehearsal took place at night and involved flight separations, aerial rejoins, Helicopter Air Refueling, and a few tasks requested by the conventional units. I was not planning to travel all the way to the southern coast because I knew the South Korean President was in the area. A small prohibited airspace surrounded him to keep aircraft like ours away. But Jethro and the team worked hard to get things together, and I didn't want to delay another day. So I made up a fake airspace entry code that would convince everyone we had permission to fly in the President's vicinity – make no mistake, we did not. I wanted to see the air refueling and would make up a reason to abort before we got too close to the President.

We were on the tanker taking fuel when the Korean National Airspace Controller called to inquire about our intentions.

"Wildhorse Four-One, Incheon Control, you are heading toward Prohibited airspace. Do not continue."

I was flying in the right seat, Jethro was in the left, and Captain Kidd was between us in the jump seat.

"Jethro, tell you what. I've seen enough tonight, so we can abort the rehearsal and turn back," I said quietly into the ICS.

The young captain would not have it. "I'll handle this. Incheon Control, this is Wild Four-One and flight; we have permission to enter the Prohibited airspace."

I could only imagine the controller's expression as he clapped back. "Wild Four-One, you do not have permission; turn away now."

I still hadn't told Jethro or the other pilots that the permission we received was fake and completely invalid. "Guys," I said, "We should turn away. I've seen all I need for tonight."

Before Jethro could speak, Captain Kidd keyed the radio. "Incheon Control, Wild-Four Two. Our PPR number is Papa Alpha Three Three Dash One Bravo. How copy?"

The Korean controller had heard enough. "Wild Four-One and flight, turn to heading three zero zero right now, or you WILL be fired upon." The real-world situation was serious. Air defense systems protecting the president would shoot us out of the sky without blinking.

"Jethro, the PPR is fake. I just let you go so you'd stick with your rehearsal plan. You've already met my objectives for tonight". I keyed my radio to speak with the tanker. "Tanker One-One, go ahead and comply with Incheon Control's instructions. We'll disconnect and break away. Thanks for the support tonight."

As we headed back to Daegu, Captain Kidd started arguing that we could have continued the mission, completely missing the point that I never intended to allow the flight to continue. Yet he continued to persist in an attempt to impress me with his knowledge. I couldn't figure out his motivations, but I intended to talk with him on the ground. No, better yet. I'd speak with Jethro and make a teaching point out of the situation. But in the meantime, we still had to navigate back to base with our team and conduct our AAR.

After the After Action Review, Jethro and I sat in the pilot's lounge, discussing the day's events over a cold beer. "Jethro, look, you're doing well, but you need to get control of your AMC. The young captain is trying to impress everyone and get noticed, but that's not what I want him to focus on. We've got an opportunity here to not only learn from this operation, but we might get a couple of recruits from the conventional units. I like what I see and would love for any of them to assess for the Regiment."

"What should I do with Captain Kidd?"

"You've got to reel him in. Please keep him in check. If you can't control a junior captain, how can I expect you to work with a colonel or a general? If he acts up again, you fail."

"Don't worry, Al, I'll handle him."

I was confident he would gain and maintain control before we flew the next day. "I know you will. Now, let's get some sleep; tomorrow is a busy day."

+++

Not everything that happens on the road is stress and hardship. Here is a funny story, but I warn you, it contains gross biological references.

My hungry stomach growled as Achmed took me to his high-rise apartment downtown in Daegu; his fiancée, Areta, had a traditional Thai dinner waiting for us. Thai in Korea? That's right, they'd met on one of his frequent trips to Pattaya, Thailand. She owned a construction company, but her manager ran the day-to-day activities, allowing her to frequent Achmed's apartment.

A wonderful woman, Areta, introduced me to her cooking, and she increased the spice and relative heat of the food she cooked daily. I like hot food and encouraged her to ratchet up the spice. "Areta, you can go hotter; I'll let you know when I reach my limit."

She smiled as she placed a large grilled Sea Bass on the kitchen table, still in its skillet. I'd never eaten a whole fish before; its presentation was artistic, and my mouth watered at the pleasing aroma. "Khun Al, I would be pleased if you would take the first portion."

I wasn't sure where to begin, so I sipped my Mekhong whiskey, biding my time to analyze how to attack the fish. Areta knew what I was thinking, so she took my fork and inserted it just behind the fish head and withdrew white, flaky meat. "Khun Al, let me help you. You will find this enjoyable, but I must warn you, this is the spiciest food I have made for you so far."

"Thank you, Areta, this looks wonderful," I said as I slid the Bass past my lips. *Mmm, the fish tastes good*, I thought. *Oh, wait, there is a little after-burn. Oh, my God, it's hot, and I mean hot.*

Achmed smiled and handed me a tall glass of cold milk to soothe the spicy burn on my lips and tongue. The burning continued for an hour or so.

I probably shouldn't tell this story because it's embarrassing, but anyone traveling a lot may relate. I'd crossed several time zones and tried to adjust to the schedule of events for Jethro's check ride. In doing so, my circadian cycle and digestive schedule were thrown askew. Other than urine, I hadn't gone to the bathroom in about four days and was uncomfortable enough to visit the Flight Surgeon for treatment.

Doctor Kevorkian, as we called him, scanned his medicine supply shelves, finding a brightly colored cardboard box containing a digestive stimulant. "Al, this ought to help. Take two of these pills with water, and you should evacuate your bowels before tomorrow's flight."

"Doc, these pills are gentle, yes? I mean, I don't need to go 'number two' while in the air, if you know what I mean."

The doctor smiled. "You'll be fine, but if you want to make sure you go sooner rather than later, take three pills."

I swallowed the tiny yellow pills before dinner, but had no result that evening or the following morning. I was concerned that five days had passed without a bowel movement, and though I was physically miserable, I felt the need to put on a positive look for Jethro's flight evaluation. I glanced at my wristwatch to gauge how much time I had before the beginning of his AMB – five hours to go.

Traffic between Achmed's apartment and the 160th compound was slow, like in any city at rush hour. We discussed the aviation weather forecast and contingencies we'd like to throw at Jethro to see his responses. He was sharp and experienced, and I did not doubt he'd perform admirably – but only time would tell.

Major Cole met me at the entrance to the briefing venue. "Al, how're things going so far? How is Jethro doing? Did you know our activities and his progress are part of the daily briefing to the Commander at USSOCOM Headquarters?"

"No, Sir, I didn't know our little operation could rise to that level. Heck, it's just training."

"Yeah, but we've got ROK SEALs, ROK Rangers, Air Force Tankers from Japan, conventional aviation units, and our aircraft. We've seen some fancy evals, but this one is for the history books."

I had to agree and looked around at the setup. I examined the presentation area to ensure it was suitable for such a visible event. We used the motor pool central bay since the hangar was occupied by several aircraft. We had about 100 folding chairs for the briefing participants, for what should be a great AMB. I slid quietly into my seat several rows back from the front and toward the middle of the pack with the rest of the Chinook pilots, which I realized was a tactical mistake as my stomach began a slow, rumbling, gurgling noise. It was time for some personal relief, but surely I could wait another hour. I looked around nervously and wanted to move from my seat to the aisle without drawing attention. However, as the primary evaluator, everyone in the room watched me for clues about how Jethro was doing.

Too late to move. Jethro began the customary time hack to begin his AMB.

"In sixty seconds, it will be 15:00 India."

One minute was plenty of time to make a minor adjustment to my wristwatch, temporarily distracting myself from my digestive conundrum.

"In thirty seconds, it will be 15:00 India."

I started to sweat as I searched the crowd for an easy exit.

"Ten, nine, eight, seven, six, five, four, three, two, one, hack, 15:00 India."

Abdominal cramps joined the next wave of tummy noises – *screw the embarrassment*. I needed to move at that moment, or I was going to soil my pants in front of 100 men and women.

Without a word, I stood abruptly and went to the nearest door. I didn't care where it led; I needed to escape the crowd, which I did, though now I found myself outdoors, no closer to the restroom. I began a light jog and passed several locked doors; I stopped to let another wave of cramps pass. *This is gonna be close*, I thought.

I worked my way around the building. The front door was locked, and my security badge didn't work, as it was rated for the Fort Campbell badge readers. I knocked frantically, and a confused Major Cole let me in.

"Al, what's wrong? Is the ride over? Are you mad at something Jethro did? He…"

I didn't mean to be rude, but I cut him off forcefully. "Sir, if I don't get to the restroom now, I'm going to shit my pants, and that will end the ride for sure." I looked around and found what I needed as I brushed past the major. The restroom was well-lit, clean, and tidy, but there was no toilet paper in either stall. "No good," I yelled as I proceeded to the ladies' room next door.

I'm embarrassed to say my ass touched the porcelain, and my bowels let go instantly. In hindsight, it shows that even with all the high-tech hardware and training, human limitations must still be accounted for when planning logistics and timelines.

+++

Jethro resumed his briefing once I returned to my seat. Now, I'd be able to concentrate without physical discomfort. I retrieved a pencil from my left arm pocket and was about to write down a radio frequency when I noticed a toilet paper roll beside the briefing podium. *That's the missing roll from the men's room.* Son of a gun, Jethro was using it to wipe a runny nose as I frantically searched for the elusive roll. A vindictive 'me' would have made his evaluation much more challenging, and vengeance would have been mine, for him causing my misery – no, I needed to let it go. This flight was going to be tough enough, especially with the weather.

Ah, the weather – the forecast called for heavy rain showers and lightning, followed by thick fog in the valleys and cloud-shrouded mountains. The environmental conditions would be nearly unflyable – too risky with our task force of dissimilar helicopters, or was it?

I stopped the Air Force Sergeant mid-sentence. "When will we see the degradation in flight conditions?"

"Sir, the cloud cover is already in place, but the first rain showers won't occur until after dark."

"So, what would the conditions be if we took off in the next two hours and hit the target around 19:00?"

"I think we're looking at 6,000 broken, with cloud tops around 30,000 feet, and visibility would remain 10 miles or better until after dark."

"Okay, gentlemen. The first contingency is that we will bump the timeline to hit the target during daylight and race ahead of the deteriorating conditions. Jethro, can we do it?"

It was easily doable if everyone was game.

Jethro continued his AMB, answered questions at the end, and queried all the crews to ensure everyone agreed with the daylight option. It was all good. The hostage rescue would go as planned as far as Jethro was concerned. I'd throw a couple of minor problems his way during execution. But if he made what I considered to be stupid decisions, I'd make him pay by inserting a major problem or two. I know it sounds like I'm an asshole, but… never mind, I am a jerk, but I wanted to ensure he was ready to lead troops in combat.

+++

With our aircraft running and communications checks complete, Jethro called Daegu Ground Control for taxi instructions to Runway Three-One Right for a departure to the south. I was flying in the right seat, performing copilot duties with Jethro in the left and our young captain in the jump seat. Dan, one of my favorite Flight Engineers, manned the right M-134 minigun. His enlisted crew was the best Echo Company could offer; we'd need their skills to take down the target ship underway.

As Jethro's right-seater, I'd be responsible for physically flying the aircraft while he navigated, operated the mission-enhancing equipment, worked the radios, and kept track of all assets. He was responsible for avoiding visual detection from early warning spotters. We felt that low-level terrain flight was our best option. The real-world danger was high-tension electrical lines crisscrossing the Korean peninsula, which posed a significant safety threat to low-flying helicopters.

Good crew coordination is a way to help mitigate risk, and contour terrain flight is no exception. "Coming down and right," I said.

Ever vigilant at the right cabin door, Dan looked below and to our right. "Clear down and right."

I simultaneously banked and descended. The valley floor rushed upward as I hugged a ridgeline outside my cockpit door. We entered a north-south running valley, and I noticed that the direction of the wind changed from that of a neutral crosswind to that of a headwind. Treetops whipped by as I increased speed to compensate for the new wind vector and match our IAS-recommended ground speed.

Jethro finished his cockpit tasks and was looking out the windshield again. "Left Seat is outside. Al, I want to bank some more time, speed up another 10 knots until I tell you."

I agreed with his strategy; gaining another thirty seconds in case the headwind worsened was prudent. "Roger, speeding up to 140 knots." Along with the new speed, I noticed several power lines running perpendicular to our course. I consciously tried to cross each set carefully to help avoid the hard-to-see tension lines. Those tended to run horizontally straight from the top of each support structure above the easy-to-see sagging transmission lines.

I have always enjoyed performing left-seat duties, but I had no real responsibilities except flight safety in the right seat. Jethro would get us to our target and home, or he would fail. I could have fun unless he made poor choices, but he was doing well for now, and I was happy.

Jethro refolded his chart, traced his finger along our route, and scribbled a few notes. "Al, we're looking good. The Apaches will split off at the next ACP and proceed to their BP on hill number three-oh-two. From there, they should be able to identify our target ship. The Delta Model Chinooks also split from the flight at the same ACP. They'll fly toward the port and insert the ROK Rangers for their mission." He paused while he tapped a few keys on his CDU. "I just completed a wind and OAT update. The Fuel/Power page looks good – no alerts."

"Roger," was all I said, and then we crossed ACP 10, the breakup point.

Dan called out the Apaches banking away before they disappeared from view down a different valley from us.

Left Gun notified us that the conventional Chinooks were also breaking off to the east.

Fifteen minutes later, Jethro selected the internal FM radio to confirm that the AH-64s were in position. "Slasher Six-One, this is Wild Four-One, confirm you've crossed phase line 'photon.'"

A beep and a rush of static preceded the answer as the cyphered communication began. "Wild Four-One, this is Slasher Six-One; we are in position and receiving tracking information of our ship, designating it as Target 'Zero-One Alpha.'"

We passed through a small terrain saddle, and our view opened up. We were now flying low over the water. Jethro alerted the crew. "Guys, we're 'feet wet,' turn on your HEEDS bottles." The Helicopter Emergency Egress Device System was a small aluminum bottle that contained compressed air for breathing underwater should our aircraft end up in the bay. Our survival vests sported an inflatable flotation collar, and we strategically stored two ready-to-go twenty-man rafts at both ends of the Chinook. Even with all of our pool survival training, I had no interest in swimming today, but, okay, back to inserting ROK SEALs onto a moving fishing vessel to rescue our Precious Cargo (PC).

"Wild Four-One, Slasher Six-One on Fox Mike, the target vessel is in sight. Prepare to copy MGRS." He paused long enough for Jethro to ready his pencil. "The boat is located at 52S CD 9595 4082, traveling 10 knots on a heading of zero-nine, zero magnetic."

Jethro repeated the coordinates to Slasher Six-One to verify that he had written them correctly.

"Read-back correct. The target is isolated from other shipping, and no other boats are within 5 miles. Also, the 110-foot-long boat hull is black, with a white superstructure and dark highlights. There is a radio mast forward of the mid-point, and two paravane stabilizer arms are on both port and starboard rails aft of the mast. How Copy?"

Jethro was busy writing when the VWS timer chimed ten minutes from TOT. "*Bing Bong – Bing Bong.*"

I alerted the crew, "Ten minutes – ten minutes," and then waited for the crew chiefs to respond.

"Ten minutes, Aft ready."

"Ten minutes, Forward ready."

Flying along 50 feet above the water was exhilarating, and I shifted in my seat to prepare for the most exciting part, the ship takedown. I glanced at my digital map. Dajeon-Ri was the last island between Target Zero-One-Alpha and us, and it was approaching fast. As we got closer, I climbed along the rising terrain.

Our crew was readying the Fast Rope at the cabin door. Typically, we'd utilize the aft FRIES bars, but to do so would require me to hold the Chinook ramp perpendicular over the bow of the moving boat in rough seas with my aft rotor blade tips mere feet from a rolling radio mast – I'm a great pilot, but nobody can do that. So, instead, we stowed our right mini-gun, allowing a Fast Rope to dangle from the external rescue hoist. What we sacrificed in self-defense, we gained in my ability to hold a position over the bow while the SEALs slid down the rope from about 25 feet above the deck.

"Bing Bong – Bing Bong."

"Six minutes," I said.

Jethro checked with the other Chinooks. "Innkeeper One-Four, we are six minutes from TOT. What is your status?"

There was no delay in his answer. "Wild Four-One, Innkeeper One-four is five minutes from TOT – all good here."

Satisfied that the mission was proceeding as planned, he returned to our role just as we crested the last hill 1,000 feet higher than the water. And there to our front was Zero-One-Alpha.

I lowered the thrust and began descending toward the surface, noting that the rough ride was due to turbulence from the approaching storm. The wind velocity picked up as it shifted from the south to the east, producing angry-looking but visually striking white caps on the water. The water was beautiful, or at least I thought so until I noticed Zero-One-Alpha was pitching and rolling atop the waves amidst the white foam – these conditions would challenge my pilot skills.

Jethro came to the same conclusion. "Al, look at the boat; she's got a wild ride in these waves. The wind kicked up some as well. She's pointed directly into it, giving us a direct crosswind of 30 knots. Heck, I don't know if this takedown is doable today. What do you think?"

I wondered if I'd ever done anything like this before. The answer was a resounding no.

Jethro announced over the radio: "Wild Four-One is assaulting target. Wild Four-Two, pick up a counterclockwise orbit and standby – Break – Slasher Six-One confirm I'm heading toward the correct target."

"Wild Four-One, continue inbound. You are on the correct boat. Good luck."

"Okay, guys, this is it. Al, take us in. Dan, don't let us hit the mast or bump the gunwales with our wheels. Let's get the SEALs on the deck."

I dug my fingers deeper into my flight gloves out of nervous habit, then began a controlled slow down. It would have been cool to whip over the deck and pull the nose up with a rapid deceleration, but my experience was showing. *Slow is smooth – smooth is fast*, I reminded myself. The hover page popped up on my inboard MFD as I passed through 40 knots. 'Bitchin Betty' reminded me I was close to the water's surface – *"Altitude Low, Altitude Low."* Without thinking, I reflexively acknowledged the VWS with my thumb and settled over the bow, looking straight down at the deck forward of the wheelhouse.

The forward rotor seemed too close to the mast as the boat pitched and rolled on the rough seas. There couldn't have been more than a few feet between us at the nearest mast tilt. I was somewhat comfortable with my position, but Dan needed a slight adjustment to get the FRIES rope in the center of the deck. Fear of hitting the boat was real, and I fought my emotions, keeping them in check.

"Al, I need you to come forward 5 feet, but hold your right."

"Roger, coming forward, five." I eased the cyclic forward, my feet lightly dancing on the directional pedals in response to the gusty crosswind. The wave action carried the boat higher during swells and dropped much lower during troughs. My left hand kept pace, moving the Thrust up and down to match the movement and maintain my altitude over the deck at 20 feet.

"Forward Four, forward three, two, one – hold your forward – hold your Right, come down one – this looks good. Hold position."

My eyes were everywhere, and I scanned quickly and effectively. Years of training were paying off. Regardless of the potential danger, I was having fun.

Dan kicked the coiled FRIES rope from our Chinook. I heard it thud on the deck, even over the aircraft noise and wind. "Deploying forward Fast

Rope. The first man is moving to the cabin door. Come left one and forward two." He waited for me to make his recommended adjustments.

Holding the position he wanted was challenging, requiring me to crane my neck to its furthest right limit.

"First man's on the rope – Roping in progress. The first man is on the deck, and the second man is on the rope – Roping in progress. Hold your right. Our position is good – hold position – Roping in progress. Ten men on the deck, roping complete."

My God, I thought, *pull the rope in so I can get some distance.*

"Sir, the rope is retrieved; you're cleared for flight."

"Coming left and up," I said.

Jethro transmitted on the Fox Mike: "Wild Four-One is coming out. We'll pick up a counterclockwise orbit to wait for exfil. Wild Four-Two join on us and maintain staggered right formation."

"Wow," I said, "that was tough."

Jethro chuckled. "Dude, you still have to hoist out the PC and exfil the SEALs with the ladder. You're just getting started."

I considered making him fly the exfil, but that would be ludicrous since he couldn't see the boat from his side of the cockpit. Even so, I was the more experienced pilot; it only made sense for me to fly.

As we orbited the boat, Jethro could watch the SEALs clear the deck and wheelhouse, and he selected track mode on the FLIR, making it possible for me to see what was occurring topside on my MFD. Several of the SEALs disappeared below deck looking for the hostage. Not long after the first man hit the down-ladder, we received a radio call that the PC was secure. Five hostage takers, or Tangos, were KIA. SSE was in progress. They'd want to exfil soon, so I pulled my helmet mic boom closer to my lips in anticipation of the call.

"Wild Four-One, Dogfish Actual, ready for exfil – One PC and Ten Eagles."

"Dogfish Actual, we are inbound now – Break – all players this net, Wild Four-One is inbound for exfil of assault force and Precious Cargo. Wild Four-Two continue to orbit."

Everyone acknowledged, and I turned inbound, returning to my original orientation and altitude. Raindrops began falling, and the wind picked up another 5 knots. The boat rocked and pitched with the whitecaps. It was worse than during the infil. I doubted I could maintain a consistent altitude over the deck as the peaks and troughs looked larger than before.

"Okay, guys, I'm beginning my approach. Talk to me."

Dan was quick to respond. "Sir, come forward 20 feet and come right five."

I did as he directed.

"Slow your forward. Come down 10 feet – Down Five, four, three, two, one. Hold your down. Hold your position. Ladder going out."

I craned my neck to the right, straining for a solid visual reference; It was tough to be sure. I could see the SEALs waiting with the newly rescued hostage. We didn't expect him to climb the rope ladder. He'd get a hoist ride.

Dan was already lowering the rescue strop, a padded flotation collar. The red canvas-covered nylon strap dangled at the end of our steel braided hoist cable. "Hoisting out, hoisting out," Dan repeated.

I was working my ass off to maintain my position. My right forearm rested on my thigh, and I worked the cyclic with only wrist movement. I tried to relax, but the swaying mast was too close to my forward rotor. The aircraft heading hold feature keeps the nose of the helicopter pointed where the pilot desires, but in these conditions, it wasn't sufficient, and my feet lightly danced on the directional pedals.

"PC is connected to the cable – Hoisting in – Hoisting in. PC is off the deck – Hoisting in. PC is 5 feet from the cabin door. Come left one – forward one. PC is at the cabin door. Hold your position."

Though the operation felt like it was taking forever, it was pretty quick. Dan and his hoist assistant were well-trained and proficient.

"PC is secure – hold position – securing hoist and deploying ladder. You're climbing. Come down, Five."

I was getting lazy and needed to tighten up my control inputs.

"Ladder is on the deck; first man is on the ladder. Come right, two. Altitude is good – the first man is on the ladder. Hold position, looking good. Hold position, second man on the ladder, first man is in the cabin door," and so it went until the entire group was onboard. "The ladder is secure, and the door plug is installed. Clear for flight."

I increased my altitude above the mast, slid away from the bow to the left, and accelerated from the boat heading north.

The Apaches were done, we were done, but we hadn't heard from the Inkeeper Chinooks. Most likely, the seaside hills blocked the line-of-sight transmissions.

"Innkeeper One-Four, this is Wild Four-One – we are off target boat heading zero one zero at 100 knots – say status."

They had completed their mission and were holding north of the port waiting for us. "Wild Four-One, Inkeeper One-Four has you in sight. Go ahead and speed up, and we'll fall into trail formation."

Jethro acknowledged, and we headed for home; I was impressed with his ability to bring conventional and SOF crews together to pull off a fairly complex mission. The weather was rapidly deteriorating, and I hoped we could stay ahead of the approaching nasty storm. I passed the time en route grilling Jethro on 160th SOPs and aviation regulations. He'd been studying, and that was for sure, though I still had one more mission for him to execute during the next cycle of darkness. I had a time-sensitive target (TST) in mind, but I was now ready to complete tonight's AAR and get a hot shower, food, and a cold beer.

+++

Morning came quickly, and I met with the commander and Achmed. Once the team arrived in the planning area, I'd drop the TST on them. They'd fly north to the P-518 Tac Zone with a company of ROK Rangers, take down a compound, find a particular laptop, and return to Daegu. I'd give them forty-five minutes to plan the mission and launch at first dark. Of course, Jethro had contingencies to negotiate, and he did. He was successful, and after this grueling week, I was very proud to call him a 160th SOAR Flight Lead.

Chapter 13

CASEVAC

Is there an intangible facet of the American military, and, more so, the special operations community, that gives men the confidence to go into harm's way in the service of our nation? In my humble opinion, it's because we make every attempt to leave no man behind, dead or alive, preferably alive. One way to do that is casualty evacuation. Whether by ground vehicle, helicopter, Tilt Rotor, or fixed-wing platform, we will come for you if you're injured, separated, or lost.

The Medevac 'Dustoff' units of the US Army have responsibilities supporting specific areas of operations. They use dedicated helicopters crewed by trained medical staff. They are very good at what they do – retrieve wounded soldiers from the battlefield and deliver them to trauma treatment facilities in their AOR.

USSOCOM's CASEVAC is an organic medical asset embedded in a special operations task force, unit, or flight. It is a means of mitigating risk-to-force by quickly evacuating casualties from their point of injury to a medical trauma facility. The 160th takes its role in supporting CASEVAC seriously. We deploy some of the military's most dedicated, highly-trained doctors and medics. Years of training and real-world fights have arguably put the Night Stalkers at the forefront of casualty evacuation and battlefield medicine. At least one helicopter is assigned as the CASEVAC 'bird on every combat mission.'

As the Flight Lead, it was my responsibility to ensure an adequate medical plan was in place. Who did I turn to? We always deployed with a senior medic and a Flight Surgeon. They researched medical facilities and hospitals in the Area of Operations (AO) and kept up with their daily operational status, level of care, and bed count. I relied on their advice on where to go if we took casualties.

+++

I recently spoke with one of my favorite and most trusted medics, C.J. Porter. His path to becoming a Night Stalker Flight Medic was typical of the organization. He grew up in Eastern Tennessee and joined the Army in 1995 as a Combat Medic. He attended Basic Training at Fort Jackson, SC, and Advanced Individual Training (AIT) at Fort Sam, Houston. He found himself assigned to the 2nd Infantry Division in South Korea.

He loved the camaraderie of the infantry and cared for his soldiers' medical needs as if they were family. Still, as with any military assignment, his time in the ROK eventually ran its course, and he moved to Fort Lewis, Washington. He attended Airborne School and eventually found himself in a twenty-man airborne surgical team at what would become Joint Base Lewis-McChord (JBLM). Although not part of USASOC, they frequently supported the Rangers and First Group SF teams. That is where C.J. was introduced to the world of special operations, and he wanted in.

After volunteering and being selected as a Night Stalker, he attended the Special Operations Combat Medic Course (SOCM) at Fort Bragg, NC. The six-month Army-run school teaches advanced combat medical treatment of battlefield trauma to special operations medics from all service branches. The Global War on Terror (GWOT) was in full swing, so after achieving SOCM certification, he breezed through the 160th Green Platoon and began his first of twenty-two deployments, starting with Afghanistan in the Spring of 2002.

Conditions at Bagram in the early 2000s were Spartan and relatively primitive. Dining facilities were scarce, hot showers were rare, and many combat missions were curtailed or minimized due to a lack of external support assets, such as AC-130 Gunships and ISR platforms. Satellite tasking focused on the soon-to-be invasion of Iraq, leaving very little coverage for us. Don't get me wrong, we were still doing direct action missions, just far fewer than we had previously. We continued flying resupply missions, intel-gathering, QRF, and CASEVAC. Until the pace of targeting picked back up, C.J. would practice his aircrew skills in addition to any medical tasks.

Kyle Faudre, the senior Flight Medic, accompanied C.J. to the flight line, explaining how their role in the helicopters had morphed since the Battle of Takur Ghar in March of 2002. As they walked through the security gate onto the 160th ramp, the sun rose over the eastern mountains of the Bagram Valley. The airfield was still in its American-run infancy with only one runway and no 'hard' facilities to run operations – tents, sandbags, and HESCO barriers were everywhere. There were no sidewalks, streetlights, or reflective belts to distract from the knowledge that the Taliban and Al Qaeda were out beyond the perimeter wire waiting to fight.

The two medics opened the cargo ramp of the nearest MH-47E in the line of four and walked inside. Aircraft tail number Four-Seven-Six sat empty with only its weapons and medical gear.

Kyle lectured as they entered the cabin. "C.J., listen closely. When shit goes wrong, and men are dying, the crew and customers will look to you for calm, proficient life-saving skills. They'll gain and maintain confidence that you'll be there to stop bleeding under fire and bring them home alive. But you can't be self-loading cargo until those particular skills are needed; You need to be a crew member and earn your seat."

C.J. took Kyle's advice to heart and trained with the Non-Rated Crew Member Standardization Instructors (NRCM SI) to become a Basic Mission Qualified (BMQ) aircrew member in all three of the Regiment's helicopter platforms. The Chinook quickly became the preferred CASEVAC platform within USSOCOM due to its speed, high altitude performance, and weather penetration capabilities. The Night Stalker medics anticipated their increased role and prepared appropriately.

Life-saving medical gear placed appropriately in the designated CASEVAC bird was standardized among the fleet and organized efficiently.

About a week into C.J.'s first deployment, I returned to Afghanistan for my second. He was already in sync with the Special Operations Medical Unit (JMAU), the base hospital, and our customers.

Flying in the lead aircraft, I don't always get to spend time with the other enlisted crews in my flight, so occasionally, I like to stop by the other 'birds' and check things out.

"C.J., what's up?"

"Hey, Sir, not much. I'm just checking my gear."

I hadn't seen the robust new setup. On my last deployment, the medics only carried an aid bag. "What have you got there?"

C.J. waved his hand over a three-foot-wide black nylon hanging bag with several pockets. "Sir, we call this the 'hanging bag' because, well, it hangs." We didn't know each other well, so he smiled nervously at his attempt at humor.

I liked everything about him.

He continued my tour. "The bag is organized by treatment: Airway, Breathing, and Circulation. So, basically, stuff to open and maintain an airway, aids to breathing, and obviously to stop bleeding." He tapped his Propaq, a small electronic patient monitor. "I can observe EKG, pulse oximeter, and other vital signs with this box."

"You have meds other than Motrin?"

"Yes Sir, I carry Morphine, Fentanyl, Valium, and Dex. My IV fluids and plasma volume expanders are here." He pointed toward an empty mount on the floor. "We carry whole blood in a refrigerated container, which sits there, with power coming from the outlet above the seat rail."

I was surprised at the advances since the early days of the war, but I really shouldn't have been. Imaginative Night Stalkers have invented new gear and techniques since the unit's origin. While I admired his setup, a group of Rangers arrived to hang Fast Ropes for the night's mission, so I left the crew to their business.

+++

I once asked C.J. how many patients he treated or how many CASEVACS he performed, but his recollections, like mine, tend to run together due to sheer numbers. But I can give you an example of a typical Night Stalker CASEVAC.

Balad, Iraq, from spring through summer of 2007, was busy by any standard, and our task force hit significant targets every night. Occasionally, we'd get a strike-to-develop target, which meant 'low-hanging fruit' or mid-level leaders or facilitators, but that's one way to develop a Target Deck. But, regardless of the bad guy hierarchy, armed men are dangerous at all times. Once designated as a Capture/Kill target, they're prioritized and hit when appropriate. This particular night was dark, even with NVGs. The moon hadn't risen yet, but with heavy cloud cover and dust whipped up by twenty to thirty-knot wind, you wouldn't see it anyway.

Before heading out to our helicopters, I told the crews that the Balad hospital had completed its recent move while we slept. It was now closer to the middle of the base, and a new aerial photo of the helipad was coming soon. In the meantime, I read new coordinates for the aircraft's IAS. I also planned to fly to the helipad and land for a quick orientation after our mission.

That night, we conducted an offset infil of forty Rangers about eight kilometers downwind of the targeted compound. The windy gusts easily masked our helicopter's noise. We probably could have inserted the assault force closer, shortening the walk, but we decided to play it safe and stick with the original HLZ. The infil was uneventful, and while the assault force walked to the compound, I led our flight of two MH-47s to the FARP at Taji. Once there, we refueled, repositioned, and shut down using only the APU to keep radios on and navigation systems aligned. When sitting in this state, we advertised a three-minute launch timeline for CASEVAC or emergency exfil.

I keyed the SATCOM radio to let the ground force know our status. "Mike Bravo-One-Six-Romeo, Sumo Two-Three flight is 'Level Two' at Taji."

"Sumo Two-Three, One-Six-Romeo is passing checkpoint seven en route to O-R-P."

I looked at my watch; they still had about fifteen minutes before hitting their Observation Rally Point. I unbuckled my seat belt and carefully tucked my shoulder straps where I could easily find them when I returned – time to take a piss.

After my short biobreak, I stretched and climbed back into the left cockpit seat just in time to hear the compound assault kick off.

With my NVGs flipped up, I could see my copilot, Charlie, drinking a Rip It energy drink. "Charlie, what flavor is that?"

"Not sure," he said as he held up the can. "They all taste the same to me."

Before I could read the label, I was drawn to the UHF radio – "Shots fired."

Before I could repeat the call for the crew, another, more sinister call came across the Net – "Eagle Down, launch the CASEVAC."

Our medic was paying attention in the back of my helicopter. I usually put the medical package in Chalk Two, but their aircraft had a minor electrical problem powering the Propaq and blood fridge; until it was fixed, 'Doc' was with me.

My crew scrambled to get into position. Charlie centered the flight controls, and I started the engine. "Left Fuel pumps are on with crossfeed open – fuel Pressure lights are out."

Curly, the crew chief stationed on the left ramp, was already in place. "Sir, ready on Number One."

"ECL to ground, One to motor." I watched the MFD engine and powertrain indications move in the correct direction. "NG is 10%. One to start." The tandem main rotors began to rotate in opposite directions and picked up speed as the left engine approached its normal operating speed.

We repeated the process on the right engine and brought the rotors to their full operating RPM. All systems and Aircraft Survivability Equipment (ASE) were up and running. So I alerted the flight. "Sumo Two-Four, Two-Three is ready for takeoff."

In less than two and a half minutes, Steve, the Pilot-In-Command of Chalk Two, Callsign Sumo Two-Four, was also ready to launch.

Taji Air Traffic Control was busy but accommodating, getting us into the air as soon as I requested to depart the airfield. "Charlie, you've got guidance to ACP Twenty-Six; that's a holding point west of the target. The firefight is ongoing, and it'll take the ground force a couple of minutes to stabilize the injured personnel and secure the HLZ. We'll probably do a couple of turns in holding while we wait to be cleared in."

Even with the suspended dust and reduced visibility, we were hauling ass, headed northwest at 160 knots. Traffic on the Fires Net streamed constantly as the Ranger JTAC, Callsign Venture One-Six, coordinated a Fire Mission from Hammer Zero-One, our AC-130.

The sound of wind-whipped sand beating against the aircraft was easy to hear as our Chinook took an environmental beating. The exterior paint would survive, but I was concerned that sand ingested into the engine inlets at such a high speed and power setting might erode our turbine blades enough to cause compressor stalls or other engine maladies. For now, the instruments indicated all was well.

"Doc, how are you doing? You ready to go?"

"Yes, Sir, I'm ready. If possible, put the stretcher under the Aft rotor at the five o'clock position when you land."

Charlie said he would do as he asked. "Al, this wind is tough. We're getting beat to shit with turbulence."

I had difficulty adjusting my CDU brightness because I couldn't get my fingers on the adjustment knob as the cockpit was bouncing sporadically with the severe turbulence. "Charlie, do the best you can. They'll be calling us soon."

"Copy that, Al. Coming right on an inbound turn."

Charlie had no sooner completed his turn when we got the call. "Sumo Two-Three, Venture One Six. You are clear to land at HLZ Cardinal, marked with IR Strobe."

Charlie began to slow for landing. The visibility was still poor, but this area of Iraq was flat with no vertical obstructions. I nervously tapped my right heel as I watched tracer fire from a nearby building. It nearly hit us, but as I like to say, miss by a mile or miss by an inch, a miss is a miss. I suppose that sort of mental bravado allowed me to stay focused while the deadly little flaming projectiles headed our way.

I smiled when I realized we'd caught the JTAC off guard. His surprise and his only lack of radio discipline occurred as we landed our blacked-out Chinook masked by the gusting wind, gunfire, and dusty visual obscurant. We nearly knocked him over on landing; he keyed his mic in surprise. "Holy shit, the CASEVAC is here."

Why yes, we are.

Meanwhile, the Rangers were pouring fire onto the enemy position as Charlie put us down right where C.J. had requested. The ramp went down, and C.J. went out to meet the Ranger medic and receive a report on the status of the injured man.

Another point of origin for enemy fire appeared at Ten O'clock. All I could do was sit back and make sure my left arm covered the gap between my chest plate and the armor seat panel in hopes that any bullet that struck me from the side would stop at my arm bone instead of penetrating my chest cavity. I'd rather lose my arm than my life.

The Rangers eliminated the threat as I waited for the casualty handover to finish.

Dan kept me informed about the ongoings in the back. "Sir, the casualty is on board, 'Doc' is working on him, and the ramp is up. We're ready to go."

Charlie transitioned to the hover page, applied full power, and climbed until about 60 feet above the rotor-induced dust cloud before accelerating toward Balad.

"Charlie, you've got Flight Director Guidance for ACP Eighty-Five. That's the new hospital helipad at Balad."

"Al, we never did a flyby or ground recon of the new hospital. We might have a hard time finding it."

"Shit. You're right. When we get closer, let's bring the altitude up a little higher to gain some situational awareness. Maybe we'll pick it out of the clutter easier."

"Roger," was all Charlie said.

It shows you why you should never put something important off until later, especially in a war zone.

I didn't want to bother C.J. while he was working, but I wanted to know what we were dealing with. "'Doc', if you've got a minute, can you talk?"

"The casualty is a Ranger sergeant with a gunshot wound resulting in penetrating chest trauma. He also took an AK round in his left hand and face."

"Is he likely to survive? At this speed, we'll be at the CASH in about five minutes."

Charlie was coaxing every bit of power the engines had to give. 'Bitching Betty' was confirming his demand. "*Torque – Torque – Torque*."

"Al, do you want me to keep up this speed? The VWS is going to keep going off at this power setting."

"Keep up the speed and just Ack her away. I'm reducing Rotor RPM to 97%, which might let you get another five knots out of this thing."

C.J. informed me that he knew the casualty. He was one of the Rangers we competed against in the first-person shooter video game CALL OF DUTY. His gamer name was 'Apple Muncher.' As I heard it, he routinely left the dining facility (DFAC) with two apples every meal. I recognized his nickname. I'm unsure what's worse, knowing the casualty or anonymity. Either way, we'd give it all we had.

"Okay, guys, the Before Landing check is complete. Balad is off the nose about 3 miles." I scanned the airfield to see if I could find an apparent hospital. "I've never seen this new helipad, so keep a sharp eye," I said.

Balad is a large airbase with two almost parallel 1,100-foot-long asphalt runways and four equidistant taxiways connecting runways 12/30 and 14/32. Most of the built-up area with offices, living quarters, and hardened shelters was northeast of runway 14/32. The hospital was among that clutter, and everything looked the same in the hazy green hues of my NVGs. I tilted my head to peek under my goggles, looking for red obstruction lights or a lit windsock. Charlie was still clipping along at 160 knots.

"Dude, you're gonna have to slow down; we're a mile out." I looked at my imagery and then pointed to our front. "If you fly down the middle taxiway, the helipad is in the middle of the clutter of tents."

Charlie slowed to a more manageable 80 knots.

Dan noticed the lighted windsock and directed us to land.

On the ground, I noticed the newly poured concrete pad was well-lit and clean as I waited for the patient transfer. C.J. deplaned to perform a medical handover with the stretcher. He'd taken time to write details on a standardized casualty card that he'd hand over so there would be no doubt about injuries and treatment.

Once 'Doc' was back on board, we repositioned to our parking area on the other side of the airbase to wait for another CASEVAC or an exfil call, which came about two hours later.

The young Ranger survived thanks to quick battlefield care and a speedy ride to a modern, well-staffed, and equipped combat surgical hospital. Quality care from a Night Stalker medic may have also played an important role.

Chapter 14

OEF-P and Wild 42

2002

On September 11, 2001, USSOCOM Task Forces Sword and Dagger fired the first shots in anger, beginning the Global War on Terror. Half a world away in the Pacific, three MH-47Es from E Company, 160th Special Operations Aviation Regiment, self-deployed 1,200 miles from Daegu to Clark Air Force Base, Manila, Philippines. The nearly ten-hour journey, mostly over water, required Helicopter air refueling provided by MC-130Ps from the 351st Special Operations Wing.

Once in Manila, the pilots and crew chiefs met their supported unit, B Company,1st BN, 1st SFG, to discuss an air movement further south supporting a pre-scheduled Joint Combined Exercise, Balanced Piston 01. Such exercises aim to improve interoperability between US and Philippine military forces. Within days, the MH-47Es repositioned 365 miles south to Mactan Air Base on the island of Cebu. Their assigned task was to support 1st SFG's mission to train, advise, and assist Philippine forces, with an emphasis on 'train' and 'advise.' Assistance, as in armed conflict with the enemy, was highly discouraged. The Philippine government was then and is now in conflict with the Abu Sayyaf Terrorist group, anti-government rebels, and pirates. Being barred from direct combat did have some gray areas. For example, US forces could help Philippine troops locate Abu Sayyaf safe havens and bases. They could conduct information campaigns and civil affairs projects to help positively influence the local population. Obviously, US Forces retained the right and, indeed, the obligation to defend themselves and their allies with deadly force if required.

Although E Company brought three Chinooks, only two flew per mission, keeping the third as a spare. As was their custom, they used the Wild Four-One and Wild Four-Two callsigns.

An ever-present factor with no direct impact on Balanced Piston was the fact that back in May, Abu Sayyaf terrorists seized 20 hostages from a

Philippine resort. Two of the hostages were American missionaries, Martin and Gracia Burnham.

Although the 1st SFG and other US forces were actively searching for the Burnhams using intelligence assets available at the time, the train and advise mission continued to be the top priority for E Company's aircrews.

With memories of 9/11 fresh, everyone was undoubtedly leaning forward, supporting anything the US ground force and their host nation partners requested. One way to make a difference in the GWOT was for 1st SFG to get onto the disputed rebel territory of Basilan Island along with Philippine Marines and SEALs. The men of the Wildhorse could make that plan a reality with multiple sorties from Cebu to Basilan, 265 miles apart. The MH-47Es had the fuel capacity to fly for over five hours unrefueled, but they still needed to 'gas up' with air refueling or take cold fuel at the military base in Zamboanga, just 20 miles north of Basilan Island.

Long nights and rainy weather made the sorties more complicated than they would have been during nicer times. Still, political pressure was on to place the last SF team on Basilan to negate the efforts of Al Qaeda's Abu Sayyaf allies as quickly as possible. On a side note, if the Burnhams were found and rescued during Foreign Internal Defense support, that would be icing on the cake, and the Night Stalkers were determined not to disappoint.

On February 21, 2002, Wild Four-One and Four-Two inserted the final SF team and resupplied all other teams in the field before heading north toward their base on the island of Cebu. It had been a long day, and aircrew chronic fatigue had set in earlier in the week. The return flight seemed tolerable because this was the last flight before the entire aviation operation would finally reposition from Cebu to Zamboanga. Support flights to Basilan would now be no longer than an hour or two in duration.

The tired crews just wanted to return to base for a hot shower and a comfortable bed, and they weren't looking forward to the upcoming air refueling sortie. HAR can be fun in the best conditions, but on an overcast night with sheets of rain pouring over windshields and turbulence tossing the refueling basket around like a dangling cat toy, made getting fuel from the tanker a desperate act of survival. You must extend your flight by mating with the tanker or end up in the Sulu Sea, far from land.

The Air Force Tankers were on time at the ARCP as usual. Regardless of the poor weather conditions, a pair of MC-130Ps, callsigns Juice Seven-One and Seven-Two, flew a perfect rendezvous and joined the fuel-thirsty helicopters on track. But having the hose in front of you is no guarantee of success, and by all accounts, the turbulence made accepting the offered fuel a near impossibility. The refueling operation took longer than usual, extending the time needed to exert physical and mental effort. Almost an hour into what should have been a twenty-minute maneuver, Wild Flight broke off from the tanker and descended to their cruising altitude of 150 feet above the water. The Flight Lead selected the low altitude because, without a visible horizon, he wanted to see the texture of the ocean to help ward off disorientation; anything higher and the waves and foam would blur away under the NVGs, leaving only varying hues of green. Nobody liked flying so near the water's surface. If an engine hiccupped at all, the remaining engine would lag somewhat, and before pilots could recover the malfunctioning motor, they'd be in the drink.

The only other option would be to separate the two Chinooks in the dark and maintain a safe distance utilizing the Air-to-Air TACAN; but Wild Four-Two had a problem with Altitude decoupling when the TACAN navigation system was the helicopter's navigation source. Wild Four-Two, tail number 471, was the last remaining aircraft to have this once fleetwide problem, and it made the undesirable decision to remain together in a tight formation a valid and fateful choice.

Rain intensified as the Chinooks passed Dumaguete and entered the Cebu Straight. Wild Four-Two closed the distance with Four-One to maintain visual cues. They just had another thirty minutes to go when Wild Four-Two got within a quarter of a rotor disk of Lead and abruptly pitched up and backed off. The crew of the lead helicopter let the Flight Lead know that Chalk Two must have a flight control or AFCS malfunction due to their erratic motions.

Twenty-five minutes from home, Chalk Two looked like it would ram Wild Four-One as it climbed and dove toward Lead before backing off as it had before.

Communication between the two pilots in command revealed that fatigue-dulled reactions and spatial disorientation were a problem. Still, they could make the remaining twenty minutes to Cebu without problems.

The two helicopters continued northbound.

Wild Four-Two unexpectedly veered left and right as it moved dangerously close to Lead again before abruptly pitching up and accelerating to 150 knots as the aircraft smashed into the water at 40 degrees nose-low. On the night of February 21, 2002, at roughly 3:00 AM, Wild Four-One witnessed an explosion just off their left side where Wild Four-Two had once been – ten men died in an instant.

+++

Over 1,000 feet lay between the water's surface and Wild Four-Two's sunken wreckage. Wild Four-One retrieved three bodies on the surface immediately after impact. The others went down with the ship, as it were. A US Navy deep-sea rescue ship rushed to the scene with a remotely operated vehicle (ROV) and retrieved most of the airframe and five bodies. Ultimately, eight of the ten aircrew's bodies were recovered, with two unaccounted for.

Families and friends mourned, but after a slight operational pause, the mission to advise and assist continued and maybe even picked up steam.

+++

Intelligence sources continued to indicate that the Abu Sayyaf Group was aligned closely with Al Qaeda, performing terrorist acts as well as rebelling against the Philippine government. During the Spring of 2002, Operation Enduring Freedom – Philippines (OEF-P) replaced the Balanced Piston exercise. Abu Sayyaf leader Abu Sabaya became the main targeting effort of the recently formed Special Operations Task Force – Philippines (SOTF-P) and Joint Task Force 510 (JTF 510). Thanks to his violent attacks against the government and civilians, he and his organization officially changed categories within the intelligence community. Finding Sabaya and rescuing the Burnhams moved up on the priority list for the Philippine military and, by association, the JTF.

Political sensitivities were on everyone's minds as operations expanded and focused on Basilan Island. Civil-military and Information Operations were three-fold: enable combat operations, increase support for the Philippine government, and reduce havens available to Abu Sayyaf.

JTF 510 would provide operational advice and direct support to the Philippines' Special Forces against terror groups. Still, it would have some limitations: US personnel were not to engage in combat. There would be a fine line between direct support and not engaging the enemy, as listed within the Mission Statement to train, advise, and assist.

+++

Wild Four-Two's loss in February was emotionally devastating, but it didn't slow down E Company's roles and responsibilities.

Operations Officer CW3 Brian Russell met replacement pilots CW3 Steve Vasek and Bill Rinserk as they left the Zamboanga airport baggage claim area with their gear and personal bags.

Vasek would later describe leaving the air-conditioned terminal. "The heat was oppressive. The air felt heavy and hard to breathe as my shirt moistened with the humidity and sweat."

Russell helped carry their bags and led them to his Bongo van. The rusty but trusty Mazda, built in 1975, may have been missing a bumper, but to Steve's satisfaction, the air conditioner worked fine.

"Brian took us to our lodging at Forward Operating Base 11," said Steve. "The reception in the bunkhouse was ice cold. Nobody would look us in the eyes. I've known these pilots for years, but they didn't want to see me. I was living proof and a painful reminder that Jody, Bart, and the rest of the crew were not coming back – they were dead."

Jokes about intermittent air conditioning, the alcoholic Aussie chef's food, cold showers, and, of course, their pet monkey lightened the uneasy mood. Steve told me he exchanged his sweaty T-shirt for a dry one and headed for the planning area to figure out his new role with OEF-P.

+++

JTF 510 coordinated with and supported all Philippine military special operations forces as they focused their efforts on Basilan Island and the surrounding waterways. The MH-47s were involved in just about every aspect of OEF-P. Not only did they infil or reposition teams onto and around Basilan, but they also performed resupply, CASEVAC, and maritime missions while avoiding direct weapons engagements with the enemy.

One particular flight described to me by CW3 Russell involved his helicopter carrying a Philippine SEAL QRF.

Boat traffic in the waters west of Basilan consisted mainly of fishermen plying their trade during the day and occasionally at night. However, nearly all the boats moving between the numerous islands in the dark were smugglers, pirates, and anti-government rebels.

The Philippine Marines and Navy SEALs used small and medium-sized patrol boats with RADAR and Fixed-Wing ISR guiding them to potential targets of opportunity. Once identified, the boat crews would intercept and run down the fleeing vessels. If they didn't heave to and relent to a Visit-Board-Search and Seizure (VBSS), the government forces would view noncompliance as a hostile act and open fire with heavy machine guns until surrender, incapacitation of the boat, or death of the crew.

Wild Four-Three's job was to loiter in the air nearby and provide an airborne Quick Reaction Force if the interdiction went poorly. Brian described his flight: "So, as usual, it was fucking dark out over the water. No clouds were in the sky, and the stars glittered like no other place I'd seen. We were trailing a 50-foot cigarette boat as he was hauling ass away from land. I stayed about 5 miles downwind and listened to the radio conversations as the patrol boat, on an intercept course, attempted a stop. The transmissions, spoken in Tagalog, were hard to follow until the cigarette boat saw the approaching ship and accelerated.

The Marines coordinated with another nearby boat to head off the fleeing vessel, but they'd escape without our intervention.

Both Philippine patrol boats had US liaisons onboard to advise and assist. All of a sudden, English hit the radio channel."

"Wild Four-Three, this is Frogman-One. Fleeing vessel with hostile intent headed west. We are in pursuit but falling behind due to the speed differential. I request that you interdict with a show of force. Get it to heave-to. How copy?"

"Frogman-One, Wild Four-Three is inbound from the southeast – target in sight – ETA – Three minutes. Be advised, we'll be at 25 feet. Keep out of our line of fire in case we need to engage."

"Frogman-One copies all."

Brian's copilot accelerated and placed the speeding vessel just below the Chinook and slightly outside the rotor disk.

Brian turned on his overt position lights and white searchlight so the driver would know he'd been caught. Not only didn't he stop, but he increased his speed. He wasn't going to outrun the Chinook under any circumstances, and now he was technically committing a hostile act under the Rules of Engagement. The aircrew didn't feel threatened, so they couldn't use deadly force; they could, however, fire warning shots in front of them.

The right gunner fired a burst of several thousand rounds from his minigun, but the fleeing crew ignored the red tracers and show of force. Brian was about to call off the interdiction when a man raised a pistol and started firing in a futile attempt to scare away the aircraft. Self-defense was allowed, and Wild Four-Three poured about a thousand 7.62 MM armor-piercing rounds into the boat's four outboard motors.

The subsequent boarding went smoothly as the self-identified pirates complied with all orders from the Philippine military. Brian returned uneventfully to Zamboanga.

Meanwhile, intelligence sources were closer than ever at locating the Burnhams as April rolled into May, and communications intercepts and visual sightings of Abu Sabaya increased. It was only a matter of time before a Philippine Ranger patrol found the hostages and conducted a hasty assault under the cover of rain. The terrorists killed Martin Burnham and a Filipina nurse as the first shots were fired, while his wife, Gracia, seriously wounded, was rescued. Abu Sabaya, along with three bodyguards, fled into the night.

+++

There is a saying in the US Special Operations Command, used mainly by the AC-130 community, "You can run, but you'll only die tired."

After Martin Burnham died, the United States brought more intelligence assets to bear to find Abu Sabaya, but it wasn't a high-tech platform or satellite that revealed his location. The months-long effort to conduct civil affairs programs had won the hearts and minds of the local populace and was about to show its worth. Several locals working with the JTF informed SF teams about Sabaya's comings and goings on Basilan Island.

His pattern of life (POL) was becoming more predictable with each passing day – enough that the Philippine SEALs found his Bangka boat, best described as a large motorized ocean-going canoe with outriggers. The next cycle of darkness would tell if the previous month's efforts had been worthwhile. Several Navy patrol boats set a picket line along Sabaya's projected route. The primary assault boat carried a team of Philippine SEALs and a US liaison (LNO) to observe, advise, and communicate with mission enablers and the Marine QRF onboard Wild Four-Three.

E Company had one set of NVGs they could spare for the LNO, whose goggles he'd lent to the SEAL commander as a goodwill gesture. Not all militaries have as robust a night-fighting capability as the US.

CW3 Vasek explained the plan to capture or kill Abu Sabaya. A local source tagged his Bangka boat with a primitive but effective tracking device, which, in theory, would lead the boat assault force (BAF) directly to his position as he transited from island to island. Wild Four-Three would orbit with the QRF a comfortable distance from stalkers and prey to avoid detection.

The night was dark, with no moon or cultural lighting. Heavy cloud cover reduced the effectiveness of their light-amplifying Night Vision Goggles, and temperatures and dew point created thermal conditions unfavorable to the MH-47's FLIR. Vasek wondered if they could find the Bangka in the wide-open waters with the technological and weather-related challenges. But he wouldn't have to wait. Not long after dark, Abu Sabaya departed as predicted toward the picket line of waiting boats. The same restrictions to visibility experienced by the JTF had to have an equal impact, impeding Sabaya's men.

Vasek listened intently to the radio traffic as an overhead platform tried to give vectors to the boat assault force. As he checked his fuel status, Philippine military radio traffic increased in quantity and intensity. Steve understood some basic Tagalog, but they were too excited for him to follow along. Something big must have happened, or so he thought.

The US LNO, Frogman-One, called Wild Four-Three and requested that they move toward his position. The Patrol boat had closed the distance to the tracking device location, but the crew and SEALs without NVGs didn't make out the silhouette of the elusive Bangka boat before running it over, splitting it in half.

Abu Sabaya wouldn't be taken alive and fired his rifle at the SEALs as his crushed boat lost buoyancy and began to sink. Multiple SEALS fired at the rebel leader, simultaneously jerking his body with each round that found its mark. While most of his men tried to swim away before capture, a few dedicated fighters went down fighting to the death.

Wild Four-Three scoured the area with a white searchlight, looking for bodies and survivors, but the SEALs had either killed or captured the

Bangka occupants. Abu Sabya, a senior leader of the Abu Sayyaf Group, died. Mission accomplished.

+++

As the Joint Task Force grew with other rotary-wing assets, the powerful MH-47s, desperately needed elsewhere, returned to Korea before follow-on operations supporting the main effort in Operation Enduring Freedom – Afghanistan.

Chapter 15

Humans in SOF Part 2

Do I miss flying? I typically answer no. Oh, maybe I miss conducting special operations missions where I put assaulters on target to rescue a hostage or retrieve a wounded comrade, but what I do miss is the people – my fellow Night Stalkers.

From the earliest days of Operation Enduring Freedom, we and our ground force customers risked our lives repeatedly with and for one another. Still, stressful life-risking activities don't happen twenty-four hours a day – every day. Some of my fondest memories come from overseas deployments; many were dangerous, but often were boring. Believe it or not, both have equal emotional bonding opportunities, usually through humor and practical jokes. You have to pass the time away from home and maintain your sanity. Laughter may be one of the best treatments for common combat zone maladies like fear, boredom, and sadness.

A guy who can spin a yarn or tell twenty dad jokes in rapid succession is someone you want to share a bunk room or tent with, but the most impactful and usually funniest people are the practical jokers. You may not be in the mood for a joke and try to avoid laughing, but funny is funny, no matter your demeanor. Combat zone comedians are a blast (no pun intended).

CW4 Rich 'Tricky' Wilson (RIP) was an excellent Chinook pilot, a family man, and a practical joker, hence his nickname.

'Tricky' was smooth and subtle. Simple things like swapping the 'm' and 'n' keys on all our computer keyboards were fun. Think about it: if you touch-type without looking, there is no effect, but if you look at the keyboard at any time and use the side-by-side keys, it's a mind game. Even more fun, he liked to get into your MS Office programs, set the spell check to autocorrect, and change commonly used words to incorrect or sometimes profanity, especially if you were writing something senior officers would see.

'Tricky' was a second-rate jokester compared to CW3 Jim Frax. Jim was probably the best I'd seen at sucking people into his world of misdirection and humor. He once put a sign on the dining facility (DFAC) at Bagram stating it was closed and patrons could get a Meals Ready to Eat (MRE) from a pallet behind the supply warehouse. Sure enough, three stacks of the not-so-tasty plastic-packed meals were around back. Hungry soldiers didn't question the legitimacy of the sign and took a meal as instructed.

I went to dinner expecting the usual wait, but no line led to the dining room, thanks to the practical joker's fake signs. Word spread quickly that most personnel missed an excellent steak and lobster meal. Revenge practical jokes entered the planning stage almost immediately, and I was glad not to share a B-Hut with Jim because the crew chiefs got their revenge. First, they placed open cans of tuna in the environmental unit that circulated air throughout the living quarters. Heated by the summer sun, the fish produced a horrible stench that permeated the sleeping quarters for weeks. When the odious stink faded, they added uncooked popcorn to the same A/C unit, which eventually popped and blew through the vents onto everyone's beds.

Jim didn't stop his humorous pranks, and as I soon learned, joke timing is not always precise but often a lucky moment, as was the case when I briefed our Task Force Commander.

We'd been planning to target a senior Al Qaeda leader who we knew was going to cross the Pakistan-Afghanistan border. Objective Eight-Ball, as I'll call him, wanted a meeting with Haqqani and Taliban representatives to coordinate attacks against US and coalition forces.

Objective Eight-Ball was on a list of strike-when-found targets, and intelligence sources embedded in his camp not only knew where he was currently but where he'd be in a week. His meeting in Barikot, Afghanistan, was within our range of operations, and I was about to present a concept of operation briefing to General McChrystal for his approval.

I rehearsed my presentation while other pilots set the stage for a professional briefing. Something was amiss. The group smiled more than usual, and I couldn't figure out why. Giggles and muffled laughs could be heard around the room. Something was funny to them yet eluded me. Was I the butt of a joke? I looked behind me – nothing. I looked around the room – nothing. I looked at my boots and pants and patted my chest pockets – nothing. "Guys, what's so funny?"

"Nothing, Al," was all they said amid more giggles.

It's definitely me, but what's going on? I thought. I hadn't seen a mirror in weeks. "Is my hair messed up?"

"Hair? No."

I was too busy to worry about my looks, even if I had some goofy issue that the guys thought was funny.

+++

Later that day, I stood in line for the DFAC lunchtime meal. Rangers in front of me were subtly pointing at me and giggling like the pilots earlier. I did another uniform check and asked about my hair, but nobody hinted at what was funny. So, I ate lunch and headed to meet with General McCrystal.

I walked into the briefing room in time for the time hack.

My XO conducted the room orientation, packet, and imagery product inventory before I stepped in front of the crowd consisting of aircrew, assault force leadership, medical personnel, and fires officers. Right across from my podium sat the Task Force Commander, General Stan McChrystal, and his staff.

I brought the intelligence officer to the podium to brief, then spoke about the overall mission. Still, even though this operation was high profile and potentially dangerous, most of the audience was smirking, including the Commander – something was up. I tried again to see my reflection on the wall-mounted plexiglass-covered map, but there was nothing.

All I could do was push on with my presentation, though as I scanned the audience, I noticed Jim Frax smiling.

He gave me a thumbs-up. So, I continued.

I've briefed McChrystal numerous times; he was always friendly and engaging. This time was different; he had a look that I can't describe.

Regardless of my uneasy feeling, I finished by fielding questions from the audience, of which there were very few.

The General shook my hand before walking out. "Good briefing, Mr. Mack."

Jim Frax stepped from the crowd, tapping his finger on the plastic-covered security badge worn around my neck about chest level.

I was shocked as I tilted the badge to look. On one side, a photo of my smiling face adorned the security badge with a red-colored stripe indicating my security clearance, and on the other, something shocking to me. Jim had slipped a Chippendale Playing card into the backside of the plastic sleeve shared by my security badge. The badge was attached to its lanyard by a small swivel, which allowed it to rotate occasionally, making my official photo visible about half the time and the King of Hearts the other.

The fifty-two playing cards Frax had were just like any ever used for poker; there were the four suites: Spades, Clubs, Diamonds, and, of course, Hearts; the significance here is that the King of this deck wasn't dressed in regal royal clothing with a crown and scepter, but was a naked, tanned, muscular male dancer posed provocatively. No wonder everyone thought it was funny. I walked around the compound the entire day, oblivious that I was sporting a naked male dancer around my neck for everyone but me to see. To this day, I can't believe anyone who knew about the prank allowed me to brief General McCrystal while the King and his scepter were prominently displayed.

Jim Frax kept up the pranks, making overseas life more tolerable, especially if you weren't the butt of his practical jokes.

Oh, and I found most of the remaining fifty-one playing cards tucked into my uniform pockets, body armor, and rucksacks over many years. Night Stalkers Don't Quit (NSDQ).

Chapter 16

The Taji Triangle

2007

From late 2006 into early 2007, Iraq was a mess. Suicide bombers, Vehicle Borne Improvised Explosive Devices (VBIED), high-profile kidnappings, and aggressive anti-aircraft ambushes were the norm as part of the twenty-four-hour and evening news cycle. The preponderance of nefarious activity occurred in the so-called Suni Triangle, a geographic area with its northernmost point near Tikrit and the base stretching from west of Ar Ramadi across Al Fallujah and running just east of Baghdad.

An offshoot of Al Qaeda, known as Al Qaeda in Iraq (AQ-I), was the main culprit for ambushes, and even if they weren't the attackers, they were building bombs and supplying other insurgent groups.

Improvised Explosive Devices (IEDs) placed along the Main Supply Routes (MSR) made travel between cities, villages, and Forward Operating Bases hazardous and costly in material, men, and morale. Mine-resistant vehicles joined the convoys, but the insurgents responded by making the explosives bigger and more sophisticated. So whenever possible, people and select supplies should be moved by air, which would avoid bombs and other explosive ordinances along the MSRs.

Critical supplies and military personnel took to the air, reducing exposure to ground attacks. Thus, a newsworthy commodity, soldiers, was excised from the news cycle. Muharib Abdul Latif al-Jubouri then directed his AQ-I fighters to redirect their attention from coalition military forces to civilians. If he couldn't hit Americans or their allies, he'd go for a big show of violence and disarray to the world. He'd already ordered the kidnapping of Western journalist Jill Carroll and peace activist Tom Fox.

Jubouri's followers not only placed car bombs in crowded markets but also used dump trucks and box trucks to increase the size of VBIEDs for spectacularly large explosions to inflict the most casualties for propaganda purposes.

+++

While news of the depraved targeting of civilians shocked a global TV audience, AQ-I still needed to affect coalition forces' ability to move around the battlefield. They needed to shoot down more aircraft, and though insurgent forces brought down several a year, they needed to ramp up air attacks.

By increasing ambushes on daily truck convoys, the enemy could harass and, in some cases, impede the delivery of fuel, spare parts, and food to remote forward operating bases. The easiest way to protect those crucial loads was to provide armed helicopter support in the form of AH-64 Apache and OH-58 Kiowa Warrior gunships. These well-armed aircraft could provide close air support, aerial observation, and reconnoitering routes ahead of the vulnerable convoys.

US gunships effectively protected trucks and HMMVs until the introduction of the triangular air ambush. It was simple and effective; Gunners established themselves in hidden fighting positions roughly a kilometer apart, forming a triangle. They could wait along established flight routes to bring down unsuspecting utility or cargo helicopters performing service flights or establish themselves along the MSRs to target the attack helicopters – either would do.

Apaches and Kiowas escorted troops and contractors at low altitudes, avoiding MANPADS but placing themselves in the engagement envelope of small arms, machine guns, and other Triple-A.

Insurgents could draw a helicopter to their site by initiating a command-detonated explosive to stop a convoy. They'd continue to direct machine guns and RPG fire at the stationary vehicles from a direction they wanted an attack helicopter to fly. Once lured, the aircraft would come under effective fire from a light machine gun, forcing the crew to instinctively turn abruptly away from the stream of tracers. Of course, the second firing position was ready for the evading aircraft to turn their way, which they inevitably did.

The second position consisted of a heavy machine gun, usually a 14.5 MM DSHK or a captured American .50 Cal. The gunner would place effective heavy-caliber fire into the helicopter to shoot it down or to scare the pilots into a hasty turn to perceived safety. If they stayed low level, which was the American TTP at the time, the second gun would drive them toward a 23 MM anti-aircraft gun with two or four barrels firing hotdog-sized bullets likely to rip a lightly-armored helicopter to pieces. If they tried to gain altitude to escape the ballistic threat, the intensifying heat and exhaust from their increased engine power in a climb made them more vulnerable to MANPADS, even with countermeasures.

A subset within the 'Sunni Triangle,' known as the 'Taji Triangle,' was designated a no-fly zone. Conventional helicopters had to go around the dangerous off-limits area. This further channeled day-to-day flight routes, unintentionally making it easier for enemy gunners to predict when and where Americans would fly. The no-fly zone had the opposite effect, bringing down more aircraft. Something had to be done with the VBIEDs and the air ambushes. The solution? Us.

+++

No matter how exciting or exhilarating a day might turn out, they all start with a mundane wake-up routine. I rolled out of bed, slipped on my flip-flops, and grabbed my towel and shaving kit before heading to the showers. I was happy to see them back in service. Convoy harassment delayed our fresh water delivery by two days, forcing us to bathe with bottled drinking water. But that minor inconvenience was now in the past as the water tanks and blivets were topped off. It was time for an actual shower before beginning my day. I carefully hung my towel on a hook outside the nearest shower stall to ensure it wouldn't fall onto the slimy, wet floor. The hot water felt good, even in the afternoon heat. I was rinsing shampoo from my eyes as I heard my name. "Al, are you in here?"

"Yeah, I'm in the shower. What's up?"

"The General wants commanders, team leaders, and Flight Leads in the executive briefing area."

"Okay. When?"

"You've got about thirty minutes, but he says it's important."

I finished my shower, shaved, and returned to my trailer for a change of clothes and coffee before meeting with the Commander.

+++

General McChrystal stood before us, wearing his camouflage uniform. I sat with the Black Hawk and Little Bird Flight Leads. The SF, SEAL, Ranger, and 160th Task Force Commander sat in an adjacent row.

McChrystal read a printed email while we settled in our seats.

As I recall, he looked up and told us that the vehicle-borne explosive devices that were going off daily in the markets and communities had to stop. "Gentlemen, the tactical mission now has a strategic flair. We've got to get the explosions off the news programs. Over the next two weeks, we'll go after the entire network of VBIED makers, suppliers, facilitators, trainers, and recruits.

"Oh, and while we're dismantling Al Jouburi's operation, we'll go after the air defenses that protect them."

A Ranger platoon leader raised his hand. "Sir, does this mean we'll enter the no-fly zone with our helicopters?"

The General looked at me and the other Flight Leads, and as best I can recall, he said, "Yes. You'll take the fight to the enemy air defenses and destroy that network. I'm guessing you guys won't have any issues with that?"

I shook my head in the negative, as did the other pilots – *This is going to be wild*, I thought.

The intelligence officer presented the enemy situation and targeting information for the initial hits. During what I'll call Operation Texas, we had over 100 targets to hit. We would strike ten simultaneously on the first night, followed nightly in sequential priority with potential follow-ons. But first, we had to set conditions by taking down a lone target 27 miles west of Taji.

Rangers based in Ramadi would conduct the assault during that period of darkness (POD). So, after McChrystal's briefing, I returned to our planning area, told the guys what I'd learned, and began the planning process for Objective #1.

Todd, the FMQ Pilot in Command of Sumo Two-Four, spoke with Scott, our imagery analyst, for mensurated satellite photos of the targeted objective. Scott was the best in the business. He was quick, accurate, and highly motivated, as was everyone in our Task Force.

Meanwhile, I spoke on the phone with Major Dave, the Ranger company commander at Ramadi. Objective Turtle, the new name for the first target, was in the middle of nowhere, surrounded by a whole lot of nothing. I take that back; it was surrounded by a flat, featureless desert with no cover or concealment, making an offset infil useless. Even under the cover of darkness, the Rangers would be detected long before their stealthy walk got within rifle range.

Dave wanted to infil to the 'X.' Speed, surprise, and violence of action should help gain an initial advantage.

I relayed the assault plan to the other pilots so we could finish our flight products and brief.

We departed Balad en route to Ramadi at first dark. The moon hadn't risen yet, so it was very dark as we flew the thirty-minute flight to HLZ Stork at the Ranger compound.

Stork was a large helipad constructed of dark gray, three-foot by three-foot aluminum panels linked together for a relatively dust-free landing in the walled FOB Ramadi courtyard. My copilot, Charlie, made his approach to the far end of the pad, leaving plenty of room for Sumo Two-Four.

Once shut down, we went inside for final coordination with the Rangers. The mission was straightforward. We'd depart as a flight of two Chinooks, each carrying forty assaulters, and land in designated HLZs near four small buildings and an oversized garage. The weather forecast was troubling, but not enough to cancel the mission. After all, Operation Texas wouldn't start until Objective Turtle was off the board.

It was windy, but the dust hadn't kicked up like the forecaster predicted. I was confident we could accomplish the mission in this cycle of darkness, so off we went. Time en route was only fifteen minutes, and since we'd already test-fired the guns, I didn't really have anything to do but tap my heel nervously and re-examine my satellite imagery as Charlie flew toward our objective, followed by Chalk Two in a loose free-cruise formation.

"Ten minutes," I announced over the intercom, expecting the usual response.

"Ten minutes – Aft ready."

"Ten minutes – Forward ready."

Major Dave stuck his head into the cockpit to acknowledge the time hack with a thumbs-up.

We repeated the time ritual at the six-minute mark and one minute out. I could make out the landing area, and Charlie could too.

"Alright, guys, the landing area is off the nose about a mile."

"Sir, landing area in sight – continue forward; you're off 100 feet. Chalk Two is at our five o'clock, three disks."

I scanned my instrument panel to make sure all systems were normal, and I had a hover page selected to pop up automatically.

"Sir, light dust forming at the ramp – you're off 40 feet."

"Charlie, your ground speed is 20, and the velocity vector is straight."

The approach terminated as he greased it on.

I keyed my floor mic switch. "Sumo Two-Three is on the ground."

"Sir, ramp is down, unloading PAX – forty Rangers off the aircraft." The crew chief was quiet for a couple of seconds before speaking again. "Ramp is up – Aft ready – Clear for Flight."

"Sumo Two-Four, Sumo Two-Three on Fox – coming out."

Charlie transitioned to his hover symbology and climbed straight up until he was clear of the dust. "Right Seat is outside," he announced as he accelerated toward Taji.

Two-Four joined us and maintained a loose free-cruise formation like earlier.

I selected my VHF radio to communicate with ATC. "Taji Tower, Sumo Two-Three is a flight of two forty-sevens 8 miles out in sector Victor at 300 feet inbound for the FARP with ATIS information Golf."

"Sumo Flight, continue inbound. Make right traffic for runway One-Six."

As Charlie turned left to enter the downwind leg of the pattern, I had the most surprising call over my SATCOM.

"Sumo Two-Three, this is Brown Zero-Six on SAT. Do you have a problem?"

The commander was calling, but I wasn't sure why. After all, the infil went well; we encountered no bad weather, Taji was out our right door, and we were about to refuel.

"Brown Zero-Six, Sumo Two-Three, we are fine. Confirm your question."

"Sumo, I thought you were going to Taji, but your beacon shows you turning north."

Ah, talk about command overreach. Big Brother was watching. Colonel Nomi was scrutinizing my helicopter's tracking beacon back at Balad.

I answered with all the sarcasm I could muster. "Brown Zero-Six, Sumo Two-Three, what you see is not an evasive maneuver but a traffic pattern. In about thirty seconds, we will turn right on the base leg, followed by another turn to the right for final. You can tell us when to begin our approach if you'd like."

Colonel Nomi was a pilot, and I could tell he was embarrassed for not realizing what was occurring on his computer screen. His only response was, "Roger."

+++

After refueling, we shut down, ready to launch at a moment's notice.

My line-of-sight radios couldn't reach the Rangers, but I could relay through the AC-130 overhead. "Hammer One-Three, Sumo Two-Three, please relay to ground force that we're at Taji – Level Two.

After a slight delay, the AC replied: "Sumo Two-Three, Hammer One-Three, words passed – Break – ground force advises, shots fired on the objective."

With bullets flying, we'd need to be ready to depart within three minutes if a CASEVAC was required, and about this time, I noticed a drop in visibility as the wind picked up, whipping sand into the air.

I climbed out of my cockpit and strolled to Chalk Two for an in-person conversation with Todd. I wanted to discuss the deteriorating conditions and how we would execute the exfil if visibility dropped below minimums.

Satisfied that we were on the same page, I returned to my Chinook, taking a pee break en route.

I heard the target secure call ten minutes later, and SSE was in progress.

Another thirty minutes passed, and Major Dave passed a SITREP to TF Headquarters on the SATCOM. There were five EKIAs. Three VBIEDs were found; two were dump trucks, and the other was a sedan. Three Military Age Males (MAMs) would come off the objective as PUCs.

The Rangers placed all enemy weapons and explosives into one area to blow it in place (BIP). Major Dave wanted the AC-130 to destroy the enemy equipment, but the collateral damage estimate (CDE) for the 105 MM encompassed a non-combatant home. They'd have to 'BIP' the contraband using C-4, which would take some time to rig. Meanwhile, the weather was worsening quickly.

I decided to risk moving forward toward the objective and leave the safety of Taji. I figured I might be ordered to return to Balad if anyone there knew how bad the weather was. If I got closer, I could coordinate the exfil with Major Dave using line-of-sight radios instead of the SATCOM, thus keeping the Colonel from recalling me prematurely.

I started to doubt my choice as we arrived near the objective and began to hold with right turns at 100 feet above the ground – Chalk Two tucked in close, flying a staggered left formation.

I coupled the altitude hold feature to make things easier on Charlie and used the radar to look for obstacles. Visibility was worsening, and I couldn't make out the horizon, so I prodded Major Dave to hurry.

The SATCOM came to life. Big Brother was still watching. "Sumo Two-Three, Brown Zero-Six. Are you holding in the vicinity of the objective?"

"Zero-Six, affirmative. We are holding to the south awaiting exfil."

Then the commander asked the question I didn't want to answer. "Sumo, what are the weather conditions at your location?"

"Zero-Six, we've got suspended dust in the air, and the wind is blowing around 30 miles per hour."

"Sumo, I figured that out. What is the visibility in miles?"

I didn't respond to the commander immediately, trying to buy the ground force time. "Mike Bravo One Six, say time to exfil."

Colonel Nomi called two more times. I couldn't hold him off any longer and let him know visibility was about an eighth of a mile. He immediately instructed me to return to base and leave the Rangers. They would remain over day (ROD), and we'd exfil them during the next cycle of darkness, weather permitting.

I argued that I was ready to exfil and had no reason to leave them. Lucky for me, Major Dave called, making the RTB call moot.

"Sumo, we're in PZ posture right now – exfil – exfil – exfil."

We collected our Rangers and headed for Ramadi. I was thankful that visibility improved somewhat as we flew over more vegetated areas and the moon climbed slowly above the now visible horizon.

The night was a success. How many innocent civilians would have died had those vehicles been put into action?

+++

Operation Texas – Night One: General McChrystal was everywhere. He began the evening by riding in my jump seat during an offset infil. When I returned to Balad for fuel, he hopped out and hitched a ride with our MH-60s as they headed to the Baghdad MSS for their mission.

My assaulters secured their objective quickly and needed me to reposition them to a follow-on target 10 miles from their location, which I did without issues – that target yielded a second follow-on, as did many of the other missions conducted that night.

The sun was rising as I landed at Balad and taxied into parking. Between our Task Force at Balad, the team at the MSS, Al Asaad, and an attached battalion from the 82nd Airborne, I believe we hit twenty-four targets – far more than the original plan – not bad for the first night.

After completing our post-flight inspection, we headed for a debrief and chow. Our last meal before retiring for the night was everyone else's breakfast. When you're hungry, it's hard to beat an omelet, made-to-order by Iraqi cooks wearing beard nets.

+++

Operation Texas – Night Two: We downed another twelve targets without follow-on missions, but removed more bomb-making equipment and air defense munitions from the board.

+++

Operation Texas – Night Three: My Chinook was unflyable and needed a new landing gear tire. I looked at Dan, my Flight Engineer. "How long?"

"Maybe thirty minutes, the aircraft jacks are locked in a conex, and the key fell in a drainage ditch."

"Really? You've got to be kidding me."

"No, Sir, the grate covering the ditch is too small for anyone to get their hands into, and the grate itself is locked into position with a padlock. We're grabbing the bolt cutters from the tool room, but the attendant was at the PX." He tossed me a Rip It energy drink. "Sir, drink this. We'll be ready to go in about thirty minutes."

I popped the tab on the can and took a sip. I'd have to wait for the maintenance guys to do their thing. My impatience would stress me out and affect the mechanics, so I sat and looked out across the base. Like the nights before, the moon was not up yet. Stars started to appear and twinkled as the day workers turned off their lights for the night.

Dan smiled when I saw him next. "Sir, the aircraft is fixed. The technical inspector (TI) is verifying the repair work and signing the logbook. We can climb aboard and start the checklist. He'll finish before we get to engine start."

Our mission was simple: pick up the Rangers at Ramadi and conduct an offset infil in a wooded grove about 8 miles west of Taji. Their objective was a series of small-walled compounds within a much larger perimeter wall.

This deployment had been one of the busiest I'd seen in quite some time, and I wondered how much longer we could maintain the high OPTEMPO. My crew was happy and healthy, but they were also tired. Dan, a senior Staff Sergeant, and FE would man the Right Gun position. Sgt Alfie McGhee would work the Left Gun; he was a crack shot with the M-134, maybe even better than Dan. I had two new crewmembers in the back: SPC Willie Falzone on the Right Ramp and Sgt Lorenzo Pile crewed the left ramp. Like most crews, these guys were professional and fun, their bravery unquestioned – flying with them was a true pleasure.

Before donning our body armor and helmets, we discussed the mission and potential contingencies. Our targeted individual wasn't a High-Value Target (HVT) on his own, but he potentially knew Al Joubouri's current 'bed-down location' (BDL). Information leading us to this man was single-sourced with no corroborating sources, so it was unlikely to bear fruit. Other targets set for near-simultaneous prosecution were more likely to pay dividends, but we had to run down all loose ends.

So, we flew to Ramadi, picked up eighty Rangers, and headed out to conduct an off-set infil, hoping for a lead that would result in the killing or capture of our notorious target, Al Jubouri. In the meantime, MH-60s from our Task Force were conducting a similar raid about 20 miles to our south while a ground assault force (GAF) hit two targets in Baghdad.

My Rangers reached their last cover and concealment roughly an hour after infil and were already assaulting their target. A 'Shots Fired' Call came across the radio almost immediately, resulting in three EKIA. Luckily, the Rangers found our targeted individual alive, hiding under his bed instead of lying dead with his cohorts. Tactical questioning, otherwise known as battlefield interrogation, began in earnest.

Twenty minutes into the SSE, I spoke with my boss, Brown Zero-Six, on the SATCOM. "All Task Force elements. Cease current operations and proceed at best speed to the Baghdad MSS for a follow-on target."

I arranged for exfil and picked up the Rangers and their PUC before heading toward Baghdad. The moon rose as I flew over Zawra Park and Saddam's Victory Arch. The crossed sword monument provided an excellent visual cue for my approach to the MSS. One of the other teams must have uncovered actionable intelligence worthy of pulling us away from our targets.

I could see the Blackhawks were already back, as were the AH and MH-6 'Little Birds.' I made sure to make my approach steep enough to land short in the compound to avoid damaging the smaller helicopters. Once, carrying twenty-six Rangers into the walled HLZ, my rotor wash spun one of the parked MH-60s, breaking a tail wheel shear pin. I was much heavier this time with forty men on board, so I made an extra effort to land a reasonable distance away and four-wheel taxi into parking.

Before our wheel chocks were in place, our refuelers rolled up in their fuel truck to top us off with jet fuel. Oh, and fuel for thought (pun intended), POL guys (fuel handlers) don't get the respect they deserve, but I've got to say ours were the best in the business.

+++

Muharib Abdul Latif al-Jubouri's location, roughly 4 miles west of Taji, would be a short flight. Chuck, the Black Hawk Flight Lead, was the overall planner. He'd already had a good look at imagery and came up with a hasty plan. Jubouri was supposed to be in one of four buildings during this period of darkness, but sources reported that he intended to move the next day. Therefore, we had to hit him before sunrise.

Chuck handed out the Grid Reference Graphics (GRG) of the target. Printed on 8 ½″ x 11″ photo paper, the macro version showed eight compounds with building numbers, one through forty-two, overlayed on one-meter satellite imagery. The micro image zoomed in on the ten-series buildings we were focusing on. The MH-60s intended to land five aircraft in various HLZs to the north and west of the Objective. I would take my two Chinooks and land to the east and southeast near buildings fourteen and fifteen. A water-filled canal running east/west just south of the target provided a natural barrier. No helicopters landing in that direction provided an apparent avenue for escape to anyone squirting from the target buildings.

With our briefings complete, I strapped into my MH-47E and set the radios for the COMMEX; Chuck started on time, and all radios worked as they should.

With the helicopter running and ready to launch, I asked Charlie if I could fly. Of course, he said yes as we traded my map for the flight controls. I waited patiently while the smaller aircraft departed in our regular order. The AH and MH-6 'Little Birds' slowly climbed over the compound wall and accelerated as five MH-60s lifted off. Once the Black Hawks cleared the wall, I 'pulled pitch' and followed with Sumo Two-Four in trail formation. Our flight had eight assaulters on each Hawk, four men on the MH-6s, and each Chinook had an ACL of forty Rangers. We'd have to rethink our business if 120 men and two dogs weren't enough to take this target.

As I cleared the last obstacles, I noticed the Tigris River to my left. The moon was nearly at its peak, with very little dust suspended in the air; visibility was unlimited. I glanced at the instrument panel clock.

Charlie alerted the crew and assaulters that we were ten minutes out.

If I were navigating, I'd tap my heels nervously, but I didn't have that luxury with both hands and feet occupied on the controls. Instead, I flexed my fingers and dug them further into my Nomex gloves. They never seemed tight enough.

Chuck checked in with the overhead stack. Darko Zero-Three provided ISR coverage and controlled the stack of support aircraft. I listened as the AC-130 joined the stack along with an armed Predator and two F-15Es. That firepower, along with our AH-6 brothers, made a formidable force.

Charlie called out the time hacks: six minutes and one minute as I searched frantically for my landing area. Darko laid down a laser point for Paladin Six-One and his Sixties. I didn't have the benefit of a 'sparkle,' but my HLZ was there to my left front. Though it took me a few seconds to ID it for sure, it was now evident. "Landing area in sight, eleven o'clock, 400 meters," I said.

McGhee saw it next. "Sir, landing area in sight. Will you put us next to the building to the left?"

"Yes, coming slightly left – beginning my approach. Charlie, set the brakes. This is a Bravo landing to the ground."

"Roger. The brakes are set. Windows closed, looks dusty."

Landings near canals and rivers usually had minimal dust, but I could see multiple tire tracks, maybe from a tractor crisscrossing the HLZ.

Falzone made the first dust call. "Sir, heavy dust is forming at the ramp; you're off 60 feet."

Charlie confirmed my speed and height above the ground as I got closer to touchdown.

Dan leaned over his minigun. "Heavy dust mid-cabin."

Then, I was alone on the ICS as both forward gunners opened fire to defend the aircraft. The M-134s roared as I applied power to flare. Braaaaap. Braaaap.

My hover velocity vector was straight, my speed was half my altitude, and I raised my nose ever so slightly as I hit 10 feet on the radar altimeter – Touchdown. "LCTs to ground, Ground Contact lights – on, Ramp clear down."

As the Rangers ran off the helicopter via the cargo ramp, the gunners continued to return fire – Braaaap. Braaap.

"Sumo Two-Three, Darko Zero Three, you have two armed squirters moving along the north wall of building fourteen, headed for you."

I acknowledged the ISR cueing, but the two runners never approached me as they turned around with our minigun fire ricocheting in their direction. My gunners didn't get them, but in avoiding us, the squirters ran while firing their weapons at the assault force. They didn't last long and became two of four EKIAs on target.

The entire helicopter assault force departed and held about 10 miles away. We'd only done two turns in holding when we got the Objective secure radio call with SSE in progress.

Long days are worth every bit of effort and pain when you hear that the primary HVT is one of the enemy killed on target.

Muharib Abdul Latif al-Jubouri, from Saladin province, kidnapper, foreign fighter facilitator, killer of civilians, and senior leader of Al Qaeda in Iraq, died running from our US Special Operations Task Force.

What is it that the AC-130 crews say? "You can run, but you'll only die tired."

+++

Our operation succeeded in disassembling the Air Ambush Network and achieved McChrystal's desire to get the nightly vehicle bombings off the news. In my humble opinion, I'd say we saved countless Iraqi civilians.

Chapter 17

19th Hole

Humans in SOF Part 3

Special Operations Forces benefit from big budgets, realistic training, and the best equipment the military can provide. Still, it is the people who make the impossible happen time and again.

Everyone has a skill or personality trait that makes living together in a combat zone enjoyable or, at the very least, tolerable. That was evident at Karshi Khanabad (K-2), Uzbekistan, and Bagram, Afghanistan, in the early years of the Global War on Terror – from 2001 to 2004.

Living conditions while deployed impact morale, so incremental improvements to shelter, food, gyms, and bathing help keep the fighting force in fighting shape. Life at K-2 started in nasty, former Soviet hardened aircraft shelters that once stored chemicals and, some say, tactical nuclear weapons. We moved from sleeping on the floor to cots; then, we traded the cold, dirty bunkers for clean, well-lit, environmentally controlled Air Force Tempur Tents and a meager mess hall serving hot chow for dinner and breakfast.

Then, during the Tora Bora campaign of 2001, we moved forward to operate out of Afghanistan's Bagram Airbase, another former Soviet shithole. We started by living in a burned-out barracks known as the Motel Six, then moved a couple of hundred meters away to a tent city. Engineers surrounded the encampment with a ten-foot-high earthen berm. Showers and a mess hall soon followed. It couldn't get much better, or so I thought.

Plywood buildings known as B-Huts replaced tents, and bunks replaced cots.

Again, could it get better?

The micro-society that inhabits a ten-man B-Hut needs a cook, a maintenance man, an inventor, an electronics whiz, and laborers to carry cases of water and wash dishes. I may have been a Flight Lead for missions, but I was the dishwasher and laborer in our living quarters, not one of the skilled hooch mates.

CW3 John Neeler was an imaginative inventor, electrician, plumber, and master of any building trade. He transformed our B-Hut into what Doug Heimbeck (RIP) named the 19th Hole, referencing the customary restaurant or bar that adorns most eighteen-hole golf courses. He built kitchen cabinets and countertops before installing a sink that drained into an already established sewage system.

John created the building infrastructure, while Doug Heimbeck and 'Achmed' Olsan cooked like five-star chefs. Doug set his bread-making machine to bake while we flew missions, creating a welcoming aroma for our return.

Bedtime for us Night Stalkers was sunrise or later, so blacked-out windows kept our sleeping quarters dark. Before nodding off, we watched a movie from our beds. We took turns selecting the pre-sleep entertainment. In the early days, we used VHS tapes before we improved our technology for DVDs.

My time in Bagram's off-duty environment showed me the softer side of the Special Operators. These men were and still are like brothers to me, and I'll never forget the time we spent together.

Chapter 18

Objective Kiona

2007

Although we'd just killed Al Qaeda in Iraq's Information Minister, Al Joubouri, and disrupted a significant bombing ring in the Taji Triangle, we were still busy trying to gain control of vital areas from enemies around Ramadi. So, if I wasn't supporting the CAG troop at the Baghdad MSS, I was out with Rangers, hitting targets nightly.

HLZ Stork was getting slippery as a drizzle coated the dusty plates that made up the helipad. The aroma of wet dust filled the air until the rain increased to a full-on downpour. My uniform clung to my skin as I walked toward the Rangers' FOB. Rain wasn't in the forecast, so I was unprepared for wet weather.

Once inside, I hung my soaked shirt over a chair back and proceeded to the commander's office to let him know we'd arrived.

Major Dave smiled when he saw me. "Al, we've got a pretty good target tonight if the weather clears. Let's go. I want to show you something."

As we walked into the planning area, he pointed to a monitor. "Look at this ISR of Objective Spoon. An OGA team hit it earlier today using vehicles. We've already received a follow-on target from the SSE at Spoon. We're naming it Objective Fork. We can hit it when the rain goes away." Then he pointed at another monitor. "But, before we go after Fork, look at this."

I focused on the large wall-mounted video screen. An overhead ISR platform followed a small heat signature floating along the Euphrates River. "Is that a man clinging to a log in the water?"

"Yes, sir," said Major Dave. "He's a squirter from Objective Spoon. He got away on a log, and he's riding the current to safety, or so he thinks."

"If we can fly, do you want to interdict him?"

Dave nodded.

"Okay, let me call Balad and speak with the weatherman."

The phone only rang once, and Sergeant Wilson, the Air Force forecaster, answered. He apologized for missing the rain forecast and informed me that the precipitation had already passed, but fast-forming fog was already dropping visibility to less than 400 meters. We'd be lucky if the fog burned off by sunrise, let alone lift for a night flight. I gave Dave the lousy news but promised him I'd keep checking to see if we had any improvements.

+++

Luckily, rooftop access provided a good vantage point to determine real-time visibility. I compared what I could or could not see to a city map loaned to me by the intel officer; I really couldn't see much. I glanced at my wristwatch before heading downstairs to wait.

My pilots monitored the ISR feed, marked the squirter's location on an aviation chart, and recalculated flight time and fuel requirements as the fast current moved him along.

Dave told me he sent a squad of Rangers to intercept the log-riding man downstream. The river might be too broad to grab him, but they might be able to shoot him. They were there to back us up. If we couldn't fly, they'd do what they could to capture or kill him. With that in mind, I returned to the roof for another look. The fog didn't seem as thick as an hour earlier, and the wind was picking up somewhat. I could still only see about 400 meters, but what I could make out was much more evident.

LTC Nomi was along for the night as the Air Mission Commander, and he rushed to the roof with a potential mission change. "Al, can you come back downstairs? Objective Kiona just showed up in Iraq."

"Who's that?"

"He's on the list of top ten targets, and he's a 'drop what you're doing, and get him' kind of guy. He usually hangs out in Iran, but with this lousy weather, sources say he feels protected from US aircraft and ISR. Supposedly, he's meeting with Al Qaeda foreign-fighter facilitators and arms suppliers. The CAG operators at Balad want to go after him with five MH-60s, but they have the same fog and visibility problems as we have here and can't launch."

I looked outward toward the east and southeast. "Sir, the rain is gone; we're just dealing with fog. Let's look at the mission planning computer we have pre-staged downstairs. I've got an idea."

+++

In previous weeks, we'd had so many missions generated or changed while we were at the Ramadi FOB that I brought a computer and printer to help with performance, route calculations, and map printing, and it was about to pay off in a big way.

I tapped away at the keys. "Sir, what are the coordinates of Objective Kiona?"

Nomi read them aloud.

My shirt was still damp from the earlier rain, and the room was silent as I calculated an ACL and a fuel requirement.

"We don't have enough fuel to get there and back. We'll need to go to Al Taqaddum Airbase for hot gas. The weather still sucks, but is favorable to TF. We'll use the Terrain Following Radar to execute a TF approach to the departure end of Runway 1-2 Left. The FARP is off to the side. Each aircraft will have its own landing location on the runway. We'll depart here with a two-minute separation. There are no towers or antennas between Ramadi and Al Taq, so we can use a TF Clearance altitude of 300 feet until we get 5 miles out, and then we'll descend to 100 feet clearance." I paused to see if anyone complained – nothing. "Alright, the approach course is one-two-zero degrees with a final speed of zero."

"Once we're both on the ground, taxi to the FARP and take on 3,000 pounds of JP-5. Once we get our fuel, we'll back-taxi, rejoin the approach end of Runway 1-2 Left, and depart at two-minute intervals. Accelerate to 120 knots and use TACAN air-to-air 23Y–86Y to maintain separation." I watched each pilot scribble notes as I continued my in-extremis briefing. "If the fog remains at our infil coordinates, we'll do a TF approach; if it burns off, we'll conduct an en route rejoin and land together." Another twenty minutes passed as I finished with the rest of the details needed to fly this mission.

I looked at Colonel Nomi for approval. "Sir, this will work. I can get the Rangers there and back. We do this kind of thing in Afghanistan often. The Sixties have the same capability, but they don't have the same experience that we do, and you'd be coordinating five helicopters in crappy weather compared to only our two. What do you say?"

Nomi was ready. "Al, your mission is approved. Get to the helicopters, and I'll call Balad to get things rolling at Al Taq."

"Yes, Sir."

+++

I looked up to my left and right. Visibility was still no better than a quarter of a mile. I started doubting that the risk was worth the reward. But as I walked closer, I noticed my aircraft appearing out of the fog and that the helipad deck plates were no longer slippery, as the dust had been washed away. Adrenalin coursed through my body. I was excited to go after such a high-level target like Kiona.

I briefed my gunners as I slipped my body armor over my head and secured the snaps and Velcro. The guys were ready, so I headed to the cockpit to get things rolling.

Once through the companionway, I grabbed the window frame and stepped over the center console, easing myself into the left seat. Art was back as my copilot, and I watched him buckle his belt and shoulder harness while I started the Auxiliary Power Unit. Once the high-pitched whine of the APU steadied, I brought the generator, hydraulics, and systems online.

We were moving through the checklist quickly in anticipation of a fast departure. The challenge and response had a rhythm to it.

"Maintenance panel – Check"

Falzone worked the switches. "Maintenance Panel Test – proper indications – going to reset – reset good."

"Parking brake – Set."

Art released and reset the brake. "Set."

"Systems – Initialize." The GPS had already found itself, so I aligned the Inertial Navigation System and turned on the ASE. "Comms, Nav, and Flight Plan load."

Art set the radios as I tapped the CDU keys to upload the navigation points and route. Both helicopters had to have the same data to ensure coördinated maneuvers and separation.

We finished the rest of the checks, and then I looked up and keyed my floor mic.

"Sumo Two-Four, this is Two-Three on Fox Mike – Engine Start."

Lorenzo was in position at the left-side engine. "Sir, ready on Number One."

"Left side fuel pumps are on – Crossfeed is open – fuel pressure low lights are off. Engine condition lever – Ground. One, to motor."

"Sir, One is clear to start."

The massive rotors began to spin, picking up speed as the turbine engine approached its operating RPMs. I started the right-side engine the same way, took all systems out of standby mode, and readied the crew for departure. I glanced at the clock, and we were making good time.

"Before Takeoff is Complete," I announced.

Before continuing, I must admit an embarrassing facet of this story. I was so excited that I directed Art to take off, knowing that Chalk Two would remain on the ground for another two minutes. Nobody questioned my timing or orders, and Art lifted into the night sky. As he cleared the final barriers and turned toward Al Taq, Nomi spoke inquisitively.

"Al, are we going to bring the Rangers along?"

"Of course," I said, suddenly realizing that the ground force was just now walking onto the helipad. *Wow, this is embarrassing, but I can still save face – This is a visibility check – Yeah, that's it.*

"Tyrant Zero-Three, Sumo Two-Three, weather check complete, returning to land. Begin loading upon touchdown."

"Sumo, Tyrant – Copy all."

Nobody on the assault force would know about my early departure until I told Major Dave at the debrief.

Art landed, the Rangers loaded, and we departed as briefed with sixteen Rangers and one dog in my helicopter and fifteen Rangers on Chalk Two.

+++

Al Taqaddum Airbase was only 18 miles to the southeast, and it only took ten minutes to arrive.

Our MMR provided terrain following cues that Art followed precisely.

"Okay, Art, looking good. The top-of-decent is approaching, and I'm selecting a 100-foot clearance altitude. Follow your cues."

"Roger, 100 C-Alt."

"Al Taq tower, this is Sumo Two-Three. I'm a single Chinook, followed loosely by Sumo-Two-Four. He'll make his own calls. We're approaching from Sector Tango at 100 feet and request a straight-in approach to Runway One-Two Left with ATIS information Yankee."

"Sumo Two-Three, Al Taq tower – we were told to expect you and approve all requests, but you need to know that the visibility is less than 200 meters. Thick fog extends from Lake Habbaniyah, obscuring both runways, and no aircraft have been able to come in or out; we've had nine attempts. The wind is 5 knots, RVR 200 meters, Runway 1-2 left – clear to land; the field is yours. Good luck.

"Okay, Art, you're looking good."

"Roger Al, I've got a slowdown cue now."

A self-generated TF approach can only slow to forty knots, which is the best case. At sixty, I deselected TF and engaged Radar Altitude Hold. Art's inboard MFD automatically displayed a hover page at forty knots and included a doghouse symbol representing the actual landing spot.

Art maneuvered the helicopter to zero ground speed so his MFD cross-hair overlayed the doghouse symbol and announced he was stable.

I selected zero feet on the altitude hold, and we descended at 300 feet per minute until the aft gear touched the ground.

"Al Taq Tower, Sumo Two-Three is on the ground; request ground taxi to FARP."

The Air Traffic Controller couldn't believe we made it. "Sumo Two-Three, I don't know what kind of Chinook you're flying, but that's an amazing machine. Be advised, you're not visible from the tower; taxi at your own risk."

I began to four-wheel taxi along the connecting taxiway and could only see the blue edge lighting outside my door, so I followed the painted centerline as closely as possible. Sumo Two-Four's on-the-ground call came over the radio while I drove to the refuel point. So far, so good.

Dan slid under his minigun and out the Right Cabin door, where he plugged a fuel hose into the aircraft's fueling receptacle and began to take on gas. The fuelers weren't happy that I kept the Rangers on board, but I didn't want them walking around in the dense fog, especially around a running helicopter. Chalk Two took fuel from the second point when we hit our fuel total. I confirmed last-minute details with Sumo Two-Four's FMQ. Todd and Kip were a solid cockpit crew, and I fully trusted them to pull off this audacious plan. Their critical task was to infil their assault force without crashing into the ground, an obstruction, and, most importantly, me.

+++

Departure from Al Taq went smoothly and without incident. A benefit of using the radar to fly in low visibility is that even if the enemy were out in yucky weather and heard us, they couldn't shoot at what they couldn't see. As I looked out my window and only saw fog and darkness, I knew I was virtually invisible.

The weather improved as we flew the 100 miles to infil. We were far from Baghdad and closer to the Iranian border than most US helicopters operated. Sumo Two-Four closed the distance once he could see us, and we continued together in formation for the last ten minutes to land.

There was no dust upon landing, only knee-high grass. So, the Rangers started patrolling even before we departed to laager at FOB Normandy. They were anxious to close the distance to Objective Kiona before being discovered. He was likely to run back to Iran with the slightest hint of Americans in the area, and the Rangers were instructed not to pursue across international borders.

My NVGs provided a good enough video to fly without the radar to FOB Normandy to wait for the exfil call. I hoped target prosecution would be quick because the sun was rising soon, and I preferred to fly my Chinook in the dark. Regardless of the timing, I could only wait patiently while the Rangers conducted business.

My SATCOM radio crackled as the ground force reached their Observation Rally Point (ORP). They'd make a final assessment of the target and begin their assault.

These missions sometimes begin with a soft knock on the front door with a quiet entry, often finding the targeted individual asleep in bed. Other times, an interpreter with a bullhorn conducts a call-out, which can result in the bad guys coming out with their hands up or an escalation of force to entice the building occupants to give up. If none of these succeed, an explosive breach may be required to gain entry, in which case, few enemy fighters survive the encounter. We wanted Kiona alive, so the soft knock was employed successfully.

In almost all missions, overhead assets, gunships, or fighters watch the Objective and protect the helicopters and assault force, but the poor weather conditions kept everything but us on the ground.

While waiting for exfil, Chalk Two developed a minor maintenance malfunction. Well, maybe not so minor…

Todd's number two flight control hydraulic system, cooler fan circuit breaker, kept popping. So, when I say minor problem, the Chinook has two redundant flight control hydraulic systems and can be flown on only one, but there is some risk to the crew if temperatures get too hot, maybe even an in-flight fire. The Flight Engineer checked wire bundles for damage while the other mechanics sprayed electrical cleaner in all cannon plugs – nothing worked.

I calculated that I could carry Chalk Two's crew and passengers along with mine in a pinch. We'd be heavy, but the morning temperature was cool, and visibility cleared fast so I wouldn't need the MMR.

Tyrant Zero-Three, the JTAC, reached me on the SATCOM. "Sumo Two-Three, this is Tyrant, Precious Cargo in hand; Three PUCs for exfil. Moving to HLZ Black: 38S NC 2400 6406 – exfil – exfil – exfil."

Todd and I had one final conversation regarding his maintenance problem. He would fly his Chinook with me as long as he promised to set it down if the hydraulic fluid temperatures exceeded limitations. I would carry the entire force and PUCs.

The sun rose as we cranked the helicopters and departed for exfil, accelerating to 140 knots.

"Tyrant Zero-Three, Sumo flight is inbound; however, all players must ride on Sumo Two-Three due to maintenance issues with Two-Four. How copy?"

"Sumo, Tyrant copies. Request you approach and land on heading three six zero. HLZ is flat and covered with grass. The location is marked with an orange panel marker. I'll pop smoke when you're 2 miles out."

Daylight flights are different than those at night. The enemy can not only hear the helicopter, but it's easy to see. I could fly very high and stay out of machine gun or RPG range, but then I'd open myself up to the still ever-present threat of a heat-seeking MANPAD homing toward my engine's heat signature. And though I had countermeasures, they weren't 100% effective for all missiles.

Low and fast was my best protective posture. The grass-covered rolling terrain lent itself to low-level contour-hugging flight. It would be like snow skiing down a mogul-covered mountain.

I decided to fly and let Art manage the IAS and navigate. The giant helicopter moved nimbly for its size. The radar altimeter indicated 10-15 feet as I banked, climbed, and descended across the minor terrain elevation changes. If the situation weren't serious, flying like this would be fun.

I take that back; this was fun.

"Art, look ahead – one o'clock – troops lying in the grass." Their newly issued ACU pattern camouflaged uniforms, colored digitally with desert sand, urban gray, and foliage green, matched nothing on Earth. Even in the tall grass, we could make them out with ease.

"Tyrant, Sumo Two-Three, we're 3 miles out; we have you in sight – pop smoke."

The disappointment in the JTAC's voice was evident. "So much for camouflage." He paused as he pulled the pin on a smoke grenade. "Popping smoke."

"Tyrant, Sumo identifies purple smoke. Panel marker in sight. Landing now."

The Rangers and their new friends headed toward the back of the Chinook.

I couldn't see the faces of the enemy fighters with hoods covering their heads, and they still wore bedclothes. Unfortunately for Kiona, his two guards slept just as soundly as he did when the Rangers approached the hide site. Now, he had the pleasure of riding with me and my crew. I hoped he didn't puke. The ride home was going to be wild.

Once we confirmed the Eagle count, we headed for Balad, increasing speed as I headed west. My first real obstacle along our path home was a set of electrical lines. Army helicopter pilots are taught from their earliest days to cross wires at a pole because often there are thinner tension wires that run level, while the thicker and easier-to-see power wires sag. Iraqi insurgents learned this quickly and began to set command-detonated improvised explosives on the tops of poles that pilots in high-traffic areas routinely flew over. As the helicopter crossed the pole, an explosion would rip it out of the sky, killing the occupants – several aircraft were brought down in this manner in the Taji Triangle. I figured we were probably too far east to employ that technique, but I was taking no chances. I rose above the wires perpendicular to my heading and immediately dropped to 10 feet with a left bank, picking up a 30-degree heading change.

Even carrying the entire load of Rangers and their PUCs, I squeezed another ten knots from the big bird.

Major Dave put on a headset and keyed the intercom. "Al, do you like NASCAR racing or Formula One?"

"Not really. Why?"

"This has to be what it feels like – the speed, the turns, the ups and downs. Heck, my stomach is in my mouth half the time – this is pretty damn fun."

My responsibility for safely getting everyone home was at the forefront of my thoughts, but he was right. This part of the flight was fun.

I worried about Chalk Two's hydraulic cooler fan problem, but Todd called to inform us that the hydraulic fluid temperature was well within the normal operating range, meaning he would likely return to Balad without requiring a precautionary landing.

Colonel Nomi patted me on the shoulder as Art made contact with Balad ATC. As a little bird pilot, he'd heard of Terrain Following Radar and the power, speed, and maneuverability of the MH-47 Chinook, but to experience it firsthand was, in his words, "Absolutely amazing. It's impossible to imagine a helicopter pulling this off."

"It didn't," I said. "We did. We leaned forward with a positive attitude using skills honed over time by our training and combat experiences."

+++

Another rewarding mission was in the books, and I was proud of my two crews. After all, I can't fly Chalk Two from Lead, and I can't fly my Chinook without my crew. I can devise bold and risky plans to accomplish dangerous, high-profile missions, but without like-minded people in the special operations community, I would have no one to lead. I'm so proud to have served with the 160th and our partner forces, and I point to the last stanza of the Night Stalker Creed: I serve with the memory and pride of those who have gone before me, for they loved to fight, fought to win, and would rather die than quit. Night Stalkers Don't Quit!

Chapter 19

Odyssey

I've always been fascinated by Homer's epic works, particularly *The Iliad* and *The Odyssey*. In my book *Razor 03, A NIGHT STALKER'S WARS*, I tried to relate my continued wartime deployments with Odysseus's exploits in combat and his journey home from war. But this story is more similar to *The Iliad*: the path to becoming a warrior and how dedication to duty, fellow soldiers, and honor, coupled with critical thinking, can overcome any enemy. Success is not always a black-and-white outcome, as there is always a cost to doing the Nation's business.

Achieving one's goals or accomplishing a risky mission always has a price – sometimes, it's just a mere inconvenience or an expenditure of personal time; other times, the cost is the loss of human life.

September 11, 2001, began my wartime journey as a Night Stalker, and I followed the example of those who came before me. Although I ended my time in the Regiment in 2013, the men I trained and fought with continued to represent our Nation honorably in many parts of the world that you may have read about or may not be aware of.

Night Stalkers, especially Chinook crews, fought in Afghanistan until its miserable ending, and they continue to support the best special operations forces around the globe. Most of what they do is still cloaked in secrecy, as it is to their benefit to remain at least partially out of sight. Sometimes, like in this book, the public gets a tiny insight into the men, women, and equipment protecting us when called upon. Just look at the open-source story from the DOD about MH-47s rescuing 100 staffers of the US Embassy in Khartoum, Sudan. Three Chinooks flew extended periods in a well-executed Non-Combatant Evacuation Order (NEO), a mission special operations forces excel at.

Mount Hope III began the Regiment's success using Chinooks in long-range, high-performance missions, such as the early flights into Afghanistan's denied territory. The mountains, towering over 20,000 feet, were a formidable obstacle, but could not stop determined Night Stalkers from achieving their goals.

The loss of Wild 42 in the Philippines is tragic in its own right, but almost as bad is that the brave crew lost their lives in the early days of Operation Enduring Freedom with hardly a mention in the news. The Abu Sayyaf terror group took a tremendous loss of their own, thanks to the Night Stalkers in the Pacific.

As far as pilots are concerned, I hope you can see from my stories what it's like to recruit and assess valuable people and then progress up to the different levels of responsibility and skill. Pilots plan and execute segments of any mission. The crew chiefs and gunners fly along and provide input regarding load plans and timelines. The flight medics are the best in the business, and Intelligence personnel, fuelers, administrative, and maintenance teams set the conditions for any flight to succeed. In the Chinook community, there are very few lift missions that the 160th does on its own, as we usually support ground assault forces to achieve their objectives. Our attack brothers may do the same or neutralize or destroy enemy elements independently, but in the end, we all work together to do our nation's business.

Families are the unsung heroes of any military organization, and the Night Stalkers are no different. As I said, doing business has a cost, and being away from loved ones, especially children, can be difficult. I loved my time in the 160th and would do it all again, maybe with some minor adjustments to priorities regarding my family. Flying Chinooks in combat was an honor I enjoyed, but that few people will experience; traveling away from home is something many more may relate to.

So, with my version of Homer's *Iliad* behind me, I'll not take for granted that my wartime exploits are done. Much like Odysseus, I took the long way home but finally returned.

Night Stalkers Don't Quit!

Glossary

AAA	Anti-Aircraft Artillery. See also ADA.
ADA	Air Defense Artillery – Weapons and equipment for actively combating air targets from the ground. See also AAA
AFSB	Afloat Forward Support Base. An aircraft carrier or LHD is used as a base of operations to launch and recover special operations missions from offshore locations.
Air Mission Commander	When two or more aircraft are operating as one flight, an air mission commander is responsible for the overall accomplishment of the air mission. He is responsible for unity of effort for the aviation task force and any other forces under his command. He assists the Flight Lead with COA development to include contingencies.
AMB	Air Mission Briefing – A briefing to pilots informing them of their mission, commander's intent, and scheme of operation.
Amphib-1	A maneuver where an MH-47 helicopter infils special operations troops and/or boats into a body of water from a ten-foot hover.
Amphib-3	A maneuver where an MH-47 helicopter infils and/or exfils a high-speed boat with crew onto a body of water using slings, fast rope, and rope ladders.
APU	Auxiliary Power Unit – A small turbine engine providing electrical power and hydraulic pressure before the helicopter's main turbine engines run.
AOR	Area of Responsibility – The geographical area associated with a combatant command

Air Control Point	A geographic position along a flight route marked by coordinates
Call Sign	Any combination of numbers or pronounceable words identifying a unit, individual, or aircraft maintaining communications, for example, Razor 03, Sumo 23, or Turbine 31.
CAAS	Common Avionics Architecture System. The pilot/user interface for MH-47G and CH-47F helicopters. The software developed by Rockwell used technological improvements to improve upon IAS (see glossary). It allows data input and flight/mission queries to assist in mission completion.
CASEVAC	Casualty Evacuation mission. Similar to MEDEVAC, but is usually embedded within a flight and is not dedicated to an entire area or theater.
CDU	Control Display Unit. Located on the MH-47 cockpit canted console. A soft-touch keypad allows pilot's data input or information queries tied to the Integrated Avionics System (IAS) and the Common Avionics Architecture System (CAAS).
CHAFF	Radar confusion reflectors, consisting of thin, narrow metallic strips of various lengths and frequency responses, and are used to reflect echoes for confusion purposes.
Charlie Pattern	A helicopter pattern used to control air traffic flow to and from an LHD.
CJSOTF	Combined Joint Special Operations Task Force. Utilizes elements of other country's military organizations. Joint represents multi-service US forces.
CRRC	Combat Rubber Raiding Craft. A rubber zodiac-style boat utilized by special operations forces for maritime infils.
Delta Pattern	A helicopter holding pattern for US Navy air-capable ships.

EOD	Explosive Ordnance Disposal.
EOS	Electro-Optical Sensor. A sensor, similar to but technologically superior to a FLIR (see glossary). It is primarily used by aircraft to see terrain, vehicles, and personnel using differential temperature and/or fused I-2 systems (NVG).
E2	Radar Exponential Elevation display used with IAS and CAAS.
Flares	Anti-missile countermeasures used to decoy infrared/ heat-seeking missiles.
Flight Lead	The FL contributes to mission analysis and develops air mission COA, Fires, support plan, and contingencies with the ground force commander. The FL backbriefs the commander and AMC, coordinates staff support and presents AMB/ OPORD. He is the flight leader, primary navigator, and is responsible for the execution of the air mission including pre-planned first-level contingencies
FLIR	Forward-Looking Infrared. A thermal imaging sensor is used primarily by aircraft to see terrain, vehicles, and personnel using differential temperatures.
FOB	Forward Operating Base.
HAR	Helicopter Air Refueling – The refueling of a helicopter in flight by a C-130 aircraft.
HAS	Hardened Aircraft Shelter – A concrete bunker used as an aircraft hangar and bomb resistant shelter.
HEEDS	Helicopter Emergency Egress Device. A small self-contained compressed air supply for emergency crew egress for a sinking helicopter. Usually carried in a flight vest pocket during overwater flight.
HLZ	Helicopter Landing Zone – A location designated for landing a helicopter.
HOS	Helicopter Oxygen System – A console that provides supplemental oxygen to aircrews above 10,000 feet MSL.

IAS	Integrated Avionics System. The pilot/user interface for MH-47E and MH-60K helicopters. The software initially created by IBM allows data input and flight/mission queries to assist in mission completion.
IED	Improvised Explosive Device.
IIMC	Inadvertent Instrument Meteorological Conditions
LHD	Landing Helicopter Dock (LHD) amphibious assault ships. Similar to an Aircraft Carrier. Launches and recovers helicopters, vertical takeoff, and landing airplanes (Harrier, F-35, and V-22). In addition to aviation operations, the 'well deck' can launch and recover Landing Craft Air Cushion, aka hovercraft (LCAC).
ISR	An aircraft, manned or unmanned, that observes areas of interest. The acronym stands for Intelligence, Surveillance, and Reconnaissance.
LNO	Liaison Officer – A unit representative who is a subject matter expert for a supported organization.
MAM	Military Aged Male.
MANPAD	Man-Portable surface-to-air missile. Examples include SA-7, HN-5, and Stinger. This heat-seeking (IR) lock-on and tracks aircraft heat sources until impact. Sometimes they are equipped with counter-countermeasures to defeat aircraft defensive decoys.
MFD	Multi-Function Display. Located on the MH-47 instrument panel. Essentially a video screen constituting a 'glass cockpit;' the MH-47E utilizes four and the MH-47G five. All flight information is presented to the pilots, and different modes of equipment are selected here from a soft-touch bezel key surrounding the unit.
MMR	The AN/AQ174B, made by Raytheon, is a pod-mounted radar equipped with multiple modes such as terrain-following (TF) and terrain-avoidance (TA), ground mapping (GM), and weather detection and avoidance (WX).

M-134 minigun	A six-barreled 7.62 MM electric 'Gatling gun' style machine gun capable of firing several thousands of rounds per minute.
M-4	A magazine-fed, 5.56 MM rifle with a collapsible stock carried by the US military.
M-9	A magazine-fed 9 MM pistol made by Berretta carried by the US military.
NVG	Night Vision Goggles. A device usually in a binocular form used to amplify ambient and artificial light in the near-infrared range to enable pilots to see in low-light conditions (Night).
ODA	Operational Detachment – Alpha. A US special forces team consisting of twelve soldiers. Their primary missions include Direct Action (DA), Unconventional Warfare (UW), and Strategic Reconnaissance (SR).
PUC	Personnel Under Control – Usually a detainee or prisoner.
RPG	Rocket Propelled Grenade. A Warsaw Pact weapon designed to destroy tanks. Has many unintended uses as a direct-fire explosive round often used against trucks, structures, and helicopters.
SECDEF	Secretary of Defense.
SERE	Survival, Evasion, Resistance, and Escape school for high-risk-of-capture personnel such as special operations forces.
TF	Terrain Following Radar. Mode used to fly low-level around, over, and through rolling or mountain terrain with limited or no visibility.
TF	Task Force – An ad-hoc organization created with units not normally assigned together working for a single commander in a unified manner.
TUG	An aircraft tractor capable of towing airplanes and helicopters. Usually painted bright yellow or flat green.

USSOCOM Special Operations Command.

USASOC United States Army Special Operations Command. An Army organization commanded by a three-star general. Subordinate units include but are not limited to Rangers, Civil Affairs, Special Forces Groups, and 160th SOAR.

VBIED Vehicle Borne Improvised Explosive Device

VI Vehicle Interdiction. A helicopter stalks a target vehicle, usually with the assistance of an aerial surveillance platform.

VSI Vertical Speed Indicator – A gauge or cockpit indication that displays an aircraft's rate of climb or descent.